MASTERING TRADE SELECTION AND MANAGEMENT

ADVANCED STRATEGIES FOR LONG-TERM PROFITABILITY

JAY NORRIS
with AL GASKILL

New York   Chicago   San Francisco   Lisbon
London   Madrid   Mexico City   Milan   New Delhi
San Juan   Seoul   Singapore   Sydney   Toronto

The *McGraw·Hill* Companies

1 2 3 4 5 6 7 8 9 10 DOC/DOC 1 6 5 4 3 2 1

ISBN   978-0-07-175498-9
MHID   0-07-175498-9

e-ISBN 978-0-07-176011-9
e-MHID   0-07-176011-3

This publication is designed to provide accurate and authoritative information in regard to the subject matter covered. It is sold with the understanding that neither the author nor the publisher is engaged in rendering legal, accounting, securities trading, or other professional services. If legal advice or other expert assistance is required, the services of a competent professional person should be sought.
—*From a Declaration of Principles Jointly Adopted by a Committee of the American Bar Association and a Committee of Publishers and Associations*

The price charts are used with permission from eSignal.com.

McGraw-Hill books are available at special quantity discounts to use as premiums and sales promotions or for use in corporate training programs. To contact a representative, please e-mail us at bulksales@mcgraw-hill.com.

This book is printed on acid-free paper.

CONTENTS

PREFACE

Our first book, *Mastering the Currency Market* (McGraw-Hill 2009), was written to provide a foundation for learning the art of discretionary trading, and it should be a prerequisite for this book. *Mastering Trade Selection and Management* focuses on helping you to collate and balance the earlier information, and to refine the trading techniques that you are likely to use for the rest of your career. Along with covering the all-important topics of trade selection and management, this book also addresses the necessity of being able to draw up a plan and stick to that plan. By helping you understand the necessity of developing your "trader's mindset," reading this book will help to protect you from your previous opinions and belief system.

The best way I know to teach someone to trade is to demonstrate to him how to trade. That's what I do three hours a day, three days a week during the London/U.S market overlap. By conducting live, interactive market exercises for my clients, pointing out trade setups and triggers in the currency markets as they are occurring during such a busy time of the day, and demonstrating how to manage these trades, I lend clients the confidence and expertise to demonstrate to themselves that they can learn to trade. That is what this book and our courses are all about: teaching you the steps and lessons it will take to prove to yourself that you can succeed in the world's most financially rewarding arena.

There is no doubt among high-level traders that you must have a subconscious belief that your trading method is going be profitable. However, no matter how much positive attitude you bring to the table, you have to have a trading method first. A trading method is a procedure that you will follow to identify first a market to trade, then the direction that the market is moving in, then a set of circumstances that lead you to focus in on a particular price level at a particular time, and finally a definite signal to initiate a position in that market. How and when you use this method to enter, manage, and exit trades will be spelled out explicitly in a document you create called a trading plan. The method you employ and your trading plan will be what many experienced traders call "your edge."

The method you choose should be robust, meaning that it needs to work in any economic environment, and it should be scalable, meaning that it will work on time frames from the shorter-term intraday on up to the monthly and weekly time frames. It needs to work in both bull and bear markets, and it needs to work in the multitude of markets that are available to investors and traders today. The method also needs to be completely independent of what you, or your friend, or your friend's broker thinks about the current or future direction of the market in question.

The method you employ needs to be able to give you the current trend for whichever slice of time you are looking at. And if by definition the method can define direction on any time frame, then it must also be able to point out at what time and at what price the direction changed. With this information, we can now measure a market's direction at any given time, particularly around those times when significant economic events are unfolding or have already taken place. This book will teach you such a method and give you the framework to measure a stock, commodity, or currency trend on a yearly, monthly, or weekly basis, or on any other time frame, in the context of the current economic environment.

Think about that for a moment. After studying the techniques taught in this book, you will be able to quantify the effects that fundamental developments such as employment, government interest-rate policy, or consumer confidence actually have on the markets you follow. You will know ahead of time what levels would need to be breached to signal a change in trend. At week's end or month's end, you can check the trends in the markets or investment vehicles you follow and know whether the current trend is holding or has changed. When the market is approaching historical support or resistance levels, such as yearly highs or lows, or long-term retracement levels, you can monitor it down to the daily or even intraday time frames to help you make decisions such as to take a portion of your position off and move your stops closer, to hedge your position with options, or to exit your position and wait for more favorable circumstances. If a sudden change occurs in the financial markets, you will have a reliable means of gauging the effects of it on any market that is of interest to you. Before any of this can happen, however, we need to demonstrate these techniques to you so that you can go on and prove to yourself how effective they are. Once you see that what we teach works, you can decide for yourself whether you want to use our methods to trade.

Doing so will entail writing out a trading plan in detail, back-testing that plan extensively, then demo trading that plan in live markets for a time that is measured not in days or weeks, but in months or even years. We know that many students will not succeed because they aren't willing to listen or write up a trading plan or patient enough to manually back-test in an organized manner by recording trades for honest evaluation. A large percentage of retail account holders fail because they don't know that they need to do all these things. However, many fail even after they know this because they won't or can't risk the resources and time required to achieve the reward, or they just aren't suited to an endeavor in which the outcome of each individual trade is unknown 100 percent of the time. A professional already has the will to succeed before she chooses the specific goal or method. It is unlikely that anyone can teach you to have that desire.

What we give you in this book is detailed step-by-step instructions on how to select a market to trade, how to determine which direction to trade that market from, what to look for prior to trading, and when to initiate a trade. We also help prepare you for the emotional challenges you will face in trading, such as letting a profit run and not exiting a trade too early, or being fearful of taking a trade signal and losing money, or, more to the point, fear of being wrong. We will teach you how to know whether you are trading with the long-term trend or counter to it, and show you how to differentiate between a trending and a countertrending market. We will also teach you what to expect when managing a trade, and prepare you for the different market scenarios that can occur while you are in a trade. You need to know exactly what to do when a trade is going your way; what to do when it's pausing, which happens often; and what to do when it seems like it's failing.

Before you move forward on your own journey, though, it's important that you absorb this book. Then move forward at a relaxed, sure pace, and use the tools and tactics we'll be teaching you as they were meant to be used. You should be in no hurry; rather, you should be comfortable in knowing that this is your journey and you can move forward at a pace that suits you. And most important, realize that the only person who can get in the way of your success is you. There is no doubt about it: trading is well over 90 percent mental, which is why we must address your own thought process and belief system before we get into methodology.

PART ONE

Market Analysis

Chapter 1

BEFORE YOU TRADE

Most new traders realize after only a few live trades that they are terrified of the markets, and this fear is a major reason why so many traders fail.

Fear and Trading

Most people aren't able to execute under the pressure that their fear creates. I've had plenty of clients admit that putting on a live trade, particularly after a losing trade—or worse, a string of losers—is one of the hardest things they've ever had to do. Is it the money that causes them so much fear? To a degree yes, particularly if they are under-capitalized to begin with, but plenty of traders tell of being just as fearful while trading micro contracts, or even when executing trades in a demo account. So it's not just the money that brings out such strong emotions. What about fear of failure? We're probably getting warmer. Failing at a vocation is a fearful thought. However, we feel that it is actually thoughts about your future that cause so much emotion.

The idea of a future life in which your computer has become your personal cash station, which is essentially what will happen if you master the art of discretionary trading, is truly the equivalent of heaven on earth for most of us. Can you imagine not having to worry about money? Imagine being in a position to help out your family, your friends, or any charity that you thought worthy. That would certainly be a good position to be in! Your life would be like one of those car commercials around the holidays where your loved ones look out the window and there is a brand-new luxury SUV parked at the perfect angle in your marble-lined driveway with a big red bow on top.

That's what you want. That's what you've been dreaming about since fourth grade, when you first found out that your parents had to work all day to get paid money to buy you shoes, put gas in the car, and save money for your tuition. And now you've found a way to get beyond all the work and worry. Now you can pay for your family to come along on your Hawaiian vacation in January. Whether you know it or not, this is how your subconscious thoughts work. Moments after you find out how trading works and how you have control over every decision and can make unlimited amounts of money, you start dreaming the near-impossible dream. But it's no longer impossible to you. There are people who do it—granted not many, but you realize that it is possible.

From that moment on, you start mentally blocking out anything that could possibly get in the way of your achieving that dream of total freedom. And that's when, rather than coming up with a sound plan to achieve such a lofty goal, you start taking wrong turns. Rather than addressing the roadblocks along the way—inexperienced mindset, improper method, no back-testing information, no trading plan, over-paying for educational services and transaction costs, and so on—you pretend that they are not there, because too often the people you go to for help in achieving this fantastic dream of total freedom are the same people who make a living from cashing checks written by you and people like you. It's human nature to agree with someone who is telling you what you want to hear, and it's not an easy thing for the average person to back up and change course once he's made even a modest investment of either time or money.

Usually it's right about the time that you actually start trading live that you start to realize that you are a long way from that dream of the holiday

Lexus in the driveway and the Hawaiian vacation, and, worse yet, you are out a bit of time and money. That cash station that you thought your computer was to become is more like a Pandora's box, with e-mails coming from this training service and that signal service about every 12 minutes. You realize that the trading course you bought didn't come with a phone number that you could call when you have questions, and your e-mail questions keep coming back with another sales pitch to upgrade to the next-level course for only $5,995.00. Are you scared? Terrified is more like it because instead of making incremental headway toward a lofty goal, you're starting to realize that you're in a position where common sense (and your spouse) is telling you to stop throwing good money after bad and accept your place in life, which is where you were before you cooked up this dream of being a trader. You now have three choices: stay scared, be depressed, or keep going down the dark, narrow tunnel you find yourself in.

Do you still want to be a trader?

If the answer is still yes, you'd better get on the right path, which means a lot of manual back-testing and then demo trading with different methods until you settle on the right method and finalize your trading plan. And while this is a good road to be on, you're still going to face mental hurdles that may be based on conditions you probably are not aware of.

Your Belief System and the Markets

"No talking politics at the dinner table" is something that many of us heard often while we were growing up. It was sound advice because it's healthier to ingest a meal in a calm, relaxed state than it is to do so while trying to fortify a political opinion or defend against someone else's. A similar statement would be appropriate for trading: "No thinking about politics when investing or trading." This is sage advice because what you happen to believe can cost you a lot of money in the marketplace. Many of you are going to have to learn to ignore your opinions if you are going to make money as a trader. While this may sound simple, it is not. Whether you realize it or not, you have an internal belief system that started developing when you were just a toddler and has been reinforced at every major event in your life.

It sounds so simple to say, "Lose your opinion, not your money," but it is not easy to do. Just ask any investor or trader who failed to act on buy signals in the U.S. stock market in the late winter of 2009 because from a political or economic standpoint, she didn't have confidence in the then-new U.S. president's administration and policies. Imagine being a professional money manager and having to explain to investors that your "opinion" kept you on the sidelines while the S&P 500 ripped off a 50 percent rally from the March 2009 low through year-end. Or worse, you tried to trade counter to the monthly trend and went short stocks or the carry trade in mid-2009, and you didn't heed the "buy" signals quickly enough when the market turned higher in mid-July of that year. Either way, if you were a professional, you would probably be out of a job.

What historical price behavior has always highlighted is the importance of using trading methods that remove the liability of your opinion. You need to understand that it would be extremely difficult, if not impossible, to keep track of every current or future event or organization that can affect a market. This is why you need an edge, or a method, that you can count on to identify the market's direction following influential events, or at the end of the day, week, or month. The trading techniques we cover in this book will provide that, and they are straightforward and simple to grasp. But we know that many traders will complicate them unnecessarily by judging them in the context of their own belief system regarding the current economy or political environment.

Another way of saying this is to say that certain readers will be looking for the tools of technical analysis to confirm their own fundamental outlook, or vice versa. Most of the time this will not work, because your own outlook—that is, your opinion—will generally shade your analysis, causing you to overlook what the chart is telling you. Nor does that approach dovetail well with Baron Rothschild's classic market advice: "Buy when there's blood in the streets," which proved apropos in 2009 and means that when you absolutely feel like the market is going to zero and you can't imagine that it can ever recover, do the hardest thing imaginable and take the next buy signal, even when your mind is screaming "Sell!" We prefer to leave it at: trade when structure—that is, support and resistance—complements price pattern. The buy signal in Exhibit 1-1 following the 2009 low in the Dow Jones Industrial Average validates this statement.

The monthly chart in Exhibit 1-1 is as black and white as it gets. The only information on the chart, other than the dates, is derived from price. The monthly open, high, low, and closing prices are the only input we have, yet look at how effectively this information can be used. The 2002

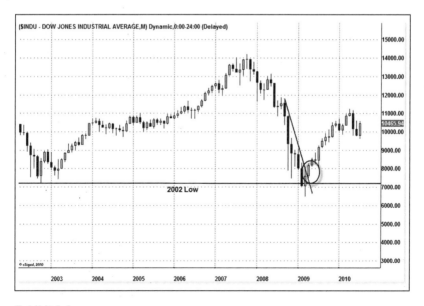

Exhibit 1-1
Source: www.esignal.com.

low is marked as potential support, and a trendline is drawn connecting the monthly highs in the second half of 2008 during an accelerated down move. Once price closes above structure—both the 2002 low and that trendline—it indicates a potential change in the price pattern, and a buy signal is given. Despite everything that was going on in the global economy, debt markets, and various governments around the world, all you really would have had to do was buy based on the knowledge that previous trendline penetrations of similar duration had, more often than not, led to sizable price moves.

This would have by no means ensured that price would move higher, because the only guarantee in trading is that the outcome of every trade is uncertain. That truism should not be discouraging, though, because the current direction of a market is definitely measurable on any time frame. While we may not know what the future holds, we do know what direction a market is moving in right now. But before we can show you that, we have to make sure that you're prepared to recognize that whatever you see will be through the lenses of your existing belief system.

We worked with a trader in 2005, and despite his having a sound understanding that oil inventories were decreasing while demand was increasing, he just couldn't bring himself to get long. Every time we showed him a buy trigger following a correction, he had a reason not to take the trade. One afternoon we were discussing the situation with the nation's strategic oil reserve, and out of the blue he started cursing the U.S. president for not releasing the reserves to try to keep down prices. "It's the right thing to do," he kept saying. I reminded him that even if that were to happen, it might have only a very short-term effect because of the substantial demand for oil from the U.S. military alone at that time, not to mention the Chinese demand. This really set him off, and as he cursed on, it suddenly hit us why he couldn't bring himself to get long oil in one of the biggest commodity bull markets of our lives.

His belief system was opposed to what was happening in the current economic environment for this commodity. Even though he had been in the energy business for many years and understood that reserves were questionable while demand was not, he was politically opposed to the prolonged war in Iraq. The fact that the U.S. president at the time was a former oilman himself only exacerbated his anger. He couldn't separate his goals as a trader from his subconscious perception (belief) that by profiting from rising oil prices, he would somehow be "a part of the problem." The moral of that story is that from a trader's perspective, "ours not to reason why."

Another example of traders getting attached to their beliefs, along with a particular market outcome, and not seeing the writing on the wall, this time on a larger scale, is what happened to so many of the "bond-market vigilantes" of the 1990s. In Chicago and New York, many proprietary trading shops that specialized in training young traders to take advantage of price movement in the U.S. Treasuries and related markets sprang up around the exchanges. Because of economic uncertainty and fear of inflation, the Treasury bond and note markets were susceptible to sell-offs that created interest-rate spikes, which were often heightened by the trading activity of these "prop" traders, who became known as "bond-market vigilantes". They called themselves this because they saw themselves as helping to establish the "true" interest rates, despite what Washington politicians said interest rates should be.

These bond-market sell-offs created volatility, which was good for the prop traders who worked on the "screen" and, like all traders, relied on market movement. It was also a boon for the futures and options traders on the floors. No one in the Treasury trading industry was complaining about the higher interest rates this collective trading activity was causing, although they created problems for the rest of the economy. However, Robert Rubin, the incoming Treasury secretary and an astute Wall Street trader himself, did notice and specifically targeted higher interest rates and the bond-market vigilantes. It did not take long for Rubin's and

Fed Chairman Alan Greenspan's lower-interest-rate policies to decimate the bond-market vigilantes who wouldn't or couldn't reverse their short positions. They became so attached to their identity as vigilantes that they overlooked the timeless Wall Street adage, "Don't fight the Fed." We remember hearing about a former bond trader who had worked for a prop shop and who had had mid-six-figure years in the past having to tell his wife that she had to go out and get a job if they were ever to have a chance of putting their kids through college.

Why couldn't the former vigilantes see that the tide had turned and that they needed to work the long side of Treasuries, or understand that lower rates might mean a weaker currency and turn to trading foreign currencies? We're not sure why, but we do know the dangers of being pigeonholed by an opinion that becomes your identity.

If other professionals can be unduly influenced by their opinions and perceived outlooks, don't believe that it can't happen to you. This is why it's important that you understand yourself first, before you start to understand how markets move. And it's even more important that you understand that your previous experiences and thoughts are going to have an outsized influence on your decision-making process if you let them. The worst thing you can do as a trader is express your opinion about the potential direction of a market that you plan on trading. This is because you literally might believe yourself, and in doing so implant an opinion in your mind that will hamper your ability to spot the subtle changes that occur before a price correction or reversal. Once you've gone on record with an opinion, you cloud your own objectivity, whether you realize it or not.

"Love is blind" is an old saying that makes a lot of sense and is applicable to trading as well because we all love being right, and getting paid for it makes it an even more dangerous aphrodisiac. Stick to fact-based assessments, such as the pattern of highs and lows in a market and the current price direction on the monthly and weekly charts, and do not fall into the trap of trying to predict a market's outcome or, worse, trying to call a "top" or "bottom" in the market. You must know that as a trader, it is never your job to predict where a market is going to go. Leave that to the analysts and financial bloggers who get paid ad dollars by the word. Your job is going to be first to secure a method that suits your lifestyle, back-test that method until you know how well it works and why it works, then finalize a trading plan to cover every contingency you can think of. After that, just stick to that plan and take the trade signals it generates, regardless of what you think the market is going to do. Then measure your progress one month at a time, not one day at a time. And stay with a demo account until your fear settles down to mild anxiety.

Why Do You Want to Trade?

The only answer to the question of why you want to trade should be to earn a satisfactory rate of return on your money while protecting your account principal. Another way of saying this is that you want to make money to have a better life. If you are trading for ego, or bragging rights, or greed, you will fail. There is an old joke in the futures industry that asks: "How do you make a small fortune trading commodities?" The answer: "Start with a big one." There are plenty of stories in the big trading families in New York and Chicago of children or grandchildren of great traders who let their egos get in the way and tried to make more than just money by making a name for themselves, which when com-bined with excessive risk ended sadly, or even tragically. There are also plenty of cases of successful businesspeople from other industries who tried their hand at trading and ended up acting like a gambling addict let loose in a casino.

It's of paramount importance that you understand that trading is a dangerous activity that can wipe out your account and leave you in debt. This is why long before you risk even 10 cents in a micro account, you had better understand that your only job as a trader is to execute your trading plan error-free with the goal of obtaining a steady rate of return on your account balance. Ideally, you should plan on being rewarded by steady returns over time. As your equity curve improves, you can add more contracts accordingly. The more contracts you trade, the greater your risk/reward scenario. Over the course of months, then years, you can amass quite a sizable account just by making modest gains week in, week out and month in, month out. This is the only reason you should want to trade.

Buyer Beware

The saying "You get what you pay for" is gospel to generations of people—particularly in America. But is it really so in the financial industry? What if we told you that it's a common belief among brokers, particularly in the more speculative futures and forex segments of the market, that the individual with the biggest, fanciest office is the best "storyteller" in that company. And the broker in that corner office is not there because he gives you a fair deal on your transaction charges/commissions. The brokers who charge you the most are generally so adept at mesmerizing their audience that clients sign up without even questioning why they are paying such exorbitant commissions.

When the average customer sees the broker's office, she gets the immediate impression that the broker must be taking good care of his customers. Why else would he be in such a nice office? It all comes back to our dream of the future. The office fits the dream. It makes perfect sense that as an up-and-coming trader, we would have a broker with such an office. He's our new friend, and he's there to help us. And he's worth every penny we pay in transaction costs because, as everyone knows, you get what you pay for! It might be hard for you to believe that a person would build his business on the strategy of seeking out prospective clients and telling them whatever they wanted to hear in order to hit his next month's commission quota. Or is it? When you are paying for services, particularly ones with such a high failure rate as retail trading, you can expect that the businesspeople behind them are going to get their fees up front. A very similar dynamic plays out in the trading education field. Fortunately, there are simple ways to find out if an educator is reputable.

First and foremost, can you get hold of the educator easily? If she doesn't have a contact phone number on her Web site or marketing material, that should raise some red flags. Another important distinction to make is whether she has some form of live trading room. Any time an educator is willing to put herself in front of you and a live market, and point out how and when a method generates trades and how to manage those trades, you can probably have some assurance that she knows what she is doing.

Just as important, educators today should also be subject to some form of regulatory review of their products and services. If you are considering purchasing educational products, there is nothing wrong with calling the educator directly and asking him if he is registered in any capacity and/or subject to regulatory review, and what form does this supervision take? From the educator's standpoint, any delay in getting products and marketing material approved by the appropriate regulatory agencies is going to be well worth the time. And educational products, like products in any service industry, should be priced for a long-term reciprocal relationship with the customer—you. If you believe that you get what you pay for in the financial trading and education industries, you need to rethink things.

Trading Corn in the Wheat Pit

Relationships change; behavior does not. The same is true of people and markets. This is something that many of us learn when we finish school or move out of our parents' home and start to live in the real world. We socialize in groups made up of friends from the old neighborhood, friends from school, and new work associates. Our friends pair up and couple off, and two people who seemed perfect for each other during the summer break up and end up avoiding each other over the holidays. A job that seems to be perfect for a particularly ambitious individual for the first few years may prove restrictive and not challenging enough after four or five years. Another friend may accept a better offer from a new firm that looks to be a great opportunity and be envied by the group, only to return to her old job for less money because she's happier there. The only constant seems to be change.

What you need to know as a trader is that markets are the same. Just as an individual is more predictable than a couple, and much more predictable than a group of people, an individual market is easier to analyze than a relationship between two markets or a group of markets. There is no doubt that at times there are powerful correlations between markets, yet just as you would not go to a group of people if you needed information from one individual, you should not analyze seemingly related markets if you are trading just one. Many new traders make the mistake of taking a trade in one market based on the behavior of another. This is a mistake, and one that we refer to as "trading corn in the wheat pit." It's very important that you know that trading should involve entering a trade in a market only if that particular market gave you a specific signal to do so. You don't want to fall into the habit of buying corn just because the price of wheat is going up. Yes, they are both grains, but there is nothing to stop one market from correcting lower while the other goes sideways, or vice versa.

The same holds with related stocks and currency markets. Experienced traders know that it is not the exception, but more to be expected that in markets that share primary trends, one will often zig while the other zags. This temporary divergence can prove costly to individuals who don't know better. And then there are those times when relationships break down completely and markets that had previously had strong correlations move in opposite directions. You will avoid the pitfalls of putting too much weight on parallel analysis of related markets by learning to enter trades or positions only because of specific price behavior, known as a setup and trade trigger, in an individual market.

Different Trade Types

There are three different trade types we will be covering, and their designation will depend on how long we plan on staying in the trade.

The first is a position trade, also called a trend trade, which we plan on holding ideally for as long as several months, to a year, or at least until the market starts to reverse against our position. We generally identify a position trade as one where the direction on the daily chart is aligned with the direction on the weekly and/or monthly chart. Our goal in being in a position trade is to move along with a markets primary trend, which we can identify as the price movement created by the current business cycle. Because we are in the market for a longer period of time, position trades have the highest risk/reward ratio.

The second is a swing trade, which we can take on any time frame chart without regard for higher time frame trends. By taking swing trades we are attempting to take advantage of the smaller trends at play in a market, sometimes called secondary price swings. The advantage of taking every swing trade signal on the chart is that you will by default end up in the biggest price moves over that time period. While swing traders may not enjoy the most impressive winning percentage, their risk/reward ratio is generally favorable.

The third type of trade is a day trade, which is a trade that would be closed out before the end of that day's trading session. As a day trader you have the choice of trading in the same direction as the higher time frame trends or swing trading. Many traders are attracted to this type of trading because of the perceived lower risk associated with trading intraday charts. As you will learn in this book, it is more important that you learn to trade from the higher time frame charts first.

Chapter 2

PREPARING TO TRADE

If you want to be a top-level trader, you have to be able to function at the top of your abilities. Finding and maintaining that tricky balance between being focused, yet relaxed for hours at a time starts with being well rested

Daily Ritual

Anything that causes you to lose focus can be detrimental to your trading, and of course a good night's sleep is very important for maintaining a positive state. Phyllis Diller, the great American comedian, used to say, "Don't ever go to bed mad . . . stay up and fight." The second part of that statement may be a punch line, but there is great wisdom in the first line. The key to waking up refreshed and feeling good is going to bed happy.

It is extremely important that you address issues in your life that are causing you doubt or stress. These can prove to be powerful distractions that can lead to problems in everything from relationships to your health. A lot of us don't get enough oxygen while we sleep because of snoring or some form of sleep apnea. Not only can this cause you to be tired upon awakening, but it can cause you to have a low attention span and lack of focus for the first hours of the day, which is a very dangerous thing for a trader. The easiest cure for this is some type of over-the-counter antisnoring mouthpieces, a number of which are available, to help you to breathe more deeply during your sleep, ensuring that you get a steady flow of oxygen into your bloodstream. Also, obvious detractors such as alcohol or caffeine should be eliminated from your routine during the trading week.

You have to ask yourself: "Am I a professional, or not?" If you don't have the discipline to pass up obvious vices that can disrupt your sleep pattern or cause you to lose focus on the job at hand, then you are not displaying the discipline and patience it takes to trade. On the trading floors, it was not uncommon for traders to stand in the pit for six hours straight with no break when there was volume moving through the markets. The stamina it took to achieve that was a natural deterrent for those who didn't have the determination and ability to participate in what was widely viewed as one of the last bastions of free commerce.

It is also not a good idea to roll right out of bed and head straight for your computer. Make it your routine to shower, dress, and go for a short walk outside before you sit down in front of the trading screen. We find that creating a space between waking up and making trading decisions helps to eliminate mental mistakes during the first hour of the trading day. During your walk, you want to imagine seeing perfect setups on the screen, with structure cradling price, then giving a signal, and the momentum following through in the direction of the higher-time-frame price pattern after you've taken the trade. You also want to practice taking deep breaths and breathing from your diaphragm, and be thankful for everything you have, especially for this new, great day!

Once you do sit down in front of the screens, do not go right to your day-trade charts. You want to start out with the monthly and weekly charts; record the short-term trend, significant structure, and recent momentum readings in your pretrade checklist spreadsheet (which we will show you how to construct shortly); and work your way down to the lower time frames. You never want to jump right into something when you can ease yourself into it. Following a consistent routine every day is going to play a big part in your trading, and will also serve as an important reminder that you are a disciplined professional.

We also need to take a look at those times when you are not physically fit to trade. Trading takes a lot of focus and a good deal more energy than you might at first realize. In fact, trading is quite demanding mentally. When you are under pressure to perform, you will become mentally drained much more quickly than you will become physically drained. All things being equal, your body will generally hold up much better than your mind. Because of this, you need to be in good shape physically and mentally, and you need to be able to admit to yourself that if you are not feeling your best in any way, you should not trade that day. That means that if you have a cold or flu, are in any kind of pain, or are on medication that might inhibit you from concentrating for hours at a time, you should not trade that day.

Likewise, you need to be mindful of your own mood. If you just had a disagreement with your spouse or your lover, you have to recognize that the emotions surging through your mind can influence your decision-making process in areas that are unrelated to that argument. Similarly, if you have to make a significant financial decision, face an unexpected setback, or have an impending expense, you had better be extra careful to follow your trading plan explicitly because the pressure you put on yourself because of these considerations can have a detrimental effect on your decision making. When it comes to trading, you need to be relaxed yet focused, confident, and above all comfortable when you sit down in front of the screens.

Your mind exerts a very powerful influence on your actions. It creates the thoughts that, in turn, influence your feelings. When you are not feeling your best, it's most likely because you are letting negative thoughts expand on themselves. You need to understand that with just a bit of effort, you can control your thoughts, but first you have to consciously notice those thoughts, track them back to where they came from, and ask yourself, "Is my thought process contributing to my being happy right now, or not?" If it isn't, then you need to think of some past event or influential person in your life that made you feel happy. If that does not work, just imagine a future event or occurrence that has a favorable outcome for you, gives you confidence, and leaves you happy. Exercises like these are going to help you to become much more in control of your thoughts and feelings. Once you experience this, you will realize what power this exercise has for putting you in the right frame of mind prior to trading. You can draw on positive feelings during those long hours on the screen when there is nothing going on.

It's crucial for you to realize that thoughts of having a successful trading day cannot come true without your knowing that you have to be patient, wait for the best trade setups and triggers, and always follow your trading plan. The times when there is nothing going on are the times when you want to consciously monitor your thoughts along with the market's price action, so that you recognize when you are getting impatient and may be reading too much into a development on the screen, or when you are getting tired and may not be noticing what is developing in the markets as much as you should.

Work Ethic

Trading is work. Once you get good at it, it can be very enjoyable—just as playing professional sports or being a professional musician must be—but long before it gets to the point where you are really enjoying yourself, it is work. Before you click that mouse and enter a trade, you are going to have to put in long hours reading and rereading this book, viewing and reviewing your course material, and, depending on whether you are a day trader and where you live, going to bed early enough to get a good night's sleep and waking up at 1 or 2 a.m. to practice trading in your demo account in live markets during the London session. And as with any job, you are going to have good days and bad days, particularly in your first couple of years, and you may have slumps during which you even doubt yourself and this dream of being a successful trader. What will carry you through these times is your work ethic. If you cannot get out of bed and prepare yourself mentally to trade after a losing day, then you are nearly assured of hanging onto the pain and confusion of a loss even longer. If you are a professional and you understand that any business has expenses, and risk, and liability, and you fully understand that if you show up for work unprepared, late, or even not at all, you will assuredly fail, then you are in a better position to succeed.

Looking at trading as work is a two-edged sword because you might at first think that because you are at your workstation on time, you should be trading. You have probably already been programmed to think that the harder you work, the more you should get paid. While this may be true in other areas, it is not the case in trading. It's your job to be patient and seek out the best trade setups and triggers with the most favorable risk/reward scenarios. And once you enter a trade, you need to know how to manage that trade without deviating from your trading plan. You need to learn to work smart, not hard. You are going to need patience, which is why so many trading coaches and authors spend so much time on teaching trading psychology. Before they can teach you to trade, they need to teach you to overcome past experiences and other distractions, and, above all, to listen.

Trading is a game of thinking before doing. It's extremely important that you be able to follow orders and stick to your plan, and more often than not, those orders and that plan will tell you to do nothing now and wait for a better setup, or to keep your stop where it is and stay in the position. Many people have a hard time listening to begin with, so it's difficult for them to follow orders, and it's nearly impossible for them to stick to a plan that someone else designed. This is why it is so important that we teach individuals to draw up their own trading plan. If you plan on your job being trading, part of working smart is creating your own trading plan.

As a short-term trader, you are going to be spending a lot of time on the screen, which, as we mentioned, is going to take a lot of energy. It's very important that you eat healthily and get a good cardiovascular workout every day. By maintaining a workout regimen, you are going to achieve a healthy physical state, which will, in turn, support your strong mental state. Trading can be a mesmerizing business for sure, and the way to break that spell and learn to be patient and wait for the high-probability setup and trigger is to maintain control of a positive thought process and keep your body as healthy as you are able.

Trading Is 99 Percent Psychological

There are only two core emotions in life: love and fear. Speculation wraps them both in the modern-day Pandora's box that is a trading platform.

When something is weighing on your mind, from a trader's perspective, it means that you are contemplating a serious distraction. What that means, in turn, is that your five senses are not fully tuned in to what is happening around you. When the mind is preoccupied, it is by definition contracting around a past distraction instead of operating as it was designed to, which is expanding outward with all the senses working at optimal levels. Distractions invoke emotions instead of vision, and judgment becomes impaired, particularly when the distraction is money. And nothing provokes that love/hate roller coaster like money. You love it when you have a pocketful of it, and you hate it when it's gone. Furthermore, you love it when you have enough of it socked away so that you don't have to worry about how you'll pay your mortgage for the next few years, and you hate it when you see your holdings contract. Nothing says you're smart and successful like driving a shiny Mercedes, and nothing makes you feel smaller than not being able to afford to go out to dinner. Money most definitely is a notorious source of unhealthy emotions. It's also the primary reason that you trade.

While money can have negative implications, such as greed, ego, and excess, losing money is even worse. Nothing evokes raw fear like losing money quickly. We know that not having a day job and losing the equivalent of one month's rent inside of 10 minutes is nothing short of terrifying.

When your average retail account holder sits down to trade, there is always something weighing on her mind. Whether it is the question of, "Will I succeed?" or "How much will I risk on this trade?" more often than not, there is some serious question at the forefront of the trader's mind at the same time that she is trying to make trading decisions. Then there are personal issues such as family, health, and environment, both real and perceived—the list could be endless. No wonder everyone is failing!

What small speculators need to realize right from the beginning is that buying and selling a market for income has nothing to do with them. Timing a market to generate profits has absolutely nothing to do with their perceptions of money or any other thing in their life or their mind. Psychology plays such a huge part in our trading only because we let it!

The first time many of us read about positive mental attitude, or PMA, we probably thought it was mumbo jumbo or psychobabble. "You mean if I think about something having a positive outcome, it will happen!?" we asked ourselves. Now that we know that this can work, many of us can't imagine an event not having a positive outcome once we apply ourselves. What you need to understand about having a positive attitude and envisioning success is how it puts us physically in the right state to be able to expand our minds and enhance our senses so that we can avoid mistakes and make the right decisions. We need to understand that the negative, restless thoughts that pop into our head have nothing to do with the reality of the current job at hand.

As traders, we have to understand that the urge to exit a trade with a small gain or a small loss despite having no signal to do so is the result of a distractive thought and has nothing to do with our thoroughly back-tested and successfully demonstrated trading method. We need to understand that if we aren't following our plan, then we are wasting our time and our money by acting on impulse. The next time you go against your plan and it costs you money, ask yourself, "Do I want to fail?" Because by listening to those negative thoughts, and not sticking to your trading plan, you are ensuring that you will fail!

And the real benefit from seeing past challenges, eliminating negative influences, and seeing success and believing that you will achieve it is the positive feelings that this creates. Envisioning real and lasting success will expand your positive thought process and kick your five senses into high gear. The optimal mindset that this creates will not only help to ensure that you are in a position to take advantage of the trading setups that you encounter, but also help you to avoid the pitfalls because of the heightened sense of awareness those positive endorphins lend your other senses. It is this positive energy that will help you to spot that intermediate-term trendline in time to protect your profit, or to stay calm and recognize that the correction against your position is lacking in momentum and you need to heed your trading plan and stay the course.

Everything that anyone has ever achieved or created started with a thought, then a vision, and the belief it could be achieved. Your success in trading will be no different. Once you've selected a trading method and manually back-tested it extensively, close your eyes and ask yourself, "Can I achieve this dream of being a successful trader?" If the answer is yes—and it should be—ask yourself what's the only thing that could stop you. Realize that the only thing that's standing in your way is yourself. And the only thing that need be on your mind when you sit down to trade—be it demo or live—is how thankful you are for the money that you're about to put into your account.

Money Management

Money management starts with a demo account, as we shall see. Once you are comfortable and, more important, showing consistency in your trading, you can move up to a live account. In the eyes of the professional trader, money management is very simple: you never risk more than X percent of your trading capital on any one trade. The number can vary from ½ of 1 percent up to 2 ½ percent, and should never be more than 2 ½ percent. Given that there are mini and micro contracts in currencies and odd lots in stocks, there is no reason why you cannot keep your risk at or under these thresholds.

The percentage risked will vary based on the trader's experience. Generally, the more experienced the trader, the smaller the percentage risked. This is because experienced traders tend to have larger accounts. The larger the account, the lower your risk should be. If you are an inexperienced trader or are brand new to trading, you need to stick to demo accounts, and your percentage risk should still be as small as possible while allowing you to trade at least two contracts at a time.

We have yet to meet a retail trader who, when asked, didn't admit that he should have spent more time in a demo account. Likewise, while we've heard from many people who insisted that they didn't learn as much in a demo account because it lacked the "feeling" of trading live money, that assertion never holds water for us. Trading is absolutely not about the "feeling of trading live money"; it's about showing up at your workstation early every day, remaining patient until you get a qualified trade setup, and executing your trading plan error-free. If you are not yet a profitable trader, when it comes to how much you are going to risk per trade, you want to stick with as small a number as you can so that you can get as many opportunities to trade as possible. Keeping your risk per trade as small as possible for your first couple of years of trading is akin to wearing a seatbelt in a car. If you have to ask why, you shouldn't be driving.

We highly recommend that if you take any tactics from this book and implement them in your own trading, you rewrite your trading plan to accommodate the changes and go back to your demo account to work on patience, trade selection, and execution. We know that money management is very important, and not using it would be akin to a pro football player's going on the field without a helmet. The reason we don't spend more ink on this subject is that we feel it is common sense, and spending more time on it would be akin to a NFL coach spending a practice session talking about the importance of wearing a helmet, instead of teaching tactics and execution.

Times *Not* to Trade

There are definitely times of the day when you should not trade, days of the week when you had better be very careful trading, namely Friday, and times of the year when you either should not trade at all or at least should trade smaller. These times are when the trader participation rates are low, and therefore volume is low. Markets nearly always behave better technically when they are moving on higher volume. The lower the volume, the more unpredictable they become because it does not take as much volume, or what traders call "size," to move the market.

For example, during a slow time of the day or month, a commercial user of a market might have to put on or adjust a hedge that had nothing to do with the user's market expectations. Perhaps a bank in Tokyo had agreed to loan a Japanese carmaker's U.S. division several hundred million dollars, but wanted to be repaid in yen. The carmaker, in turn, wanted to avoid the currency exposure, so it hedged the position in the interbank market. This transaction occurred in late July, which is traditionally a slow time of the year for the financial markets. If the carmaker didn't understand that the markets were slow and tried to hedge the entire position all at once, particularly during a slow time of the day, it would probably be disruptive to the market and create an outsized move relative to the previous trading day's range, which might cause a shift in the daily or even the weekly trend. It's because of inevitable situations like these in the financial marketplace that you want to use stop loss orders if you are a swing trader or position trader, or even if you are a day trader and you step away from the screen for a moment.

Let's start out with what times of the day not to trade, and remember that these are going to be times when there is low volume in the market. The chart in Exhibit 2-1, with volume figures in the bottom panel, makes it quite clear when to trade and when not to trade on an hour-by-hour basis. Volume picks up during the Tokyo afternoon session and increases into the London session before tapering off for lunch in London, then picking up again on the London/U.S. overlap before trailing off just

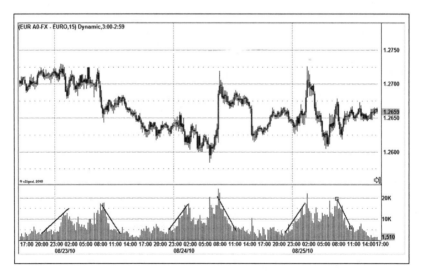

Exhibit 2-1
Source: www.esignal.com.

ahead of lunch in New York. This daily pattern is very consistent. What this means for short-term traders and day traders is, don't trade from lunchtime in New York through lunchtime in Tokyo.

Exhibit 2-1 is from August of 2010, and Exhibit 2-2 is from May of 2010. We can see the same volume pattern in each chart, and we can assure you that regardless of what time of year you pull an intraday chart of an actively traded currency, you will see the same volume pattern. As an intraday trader or day trader, you essentially do not want to trade from lunchtime in New York through lunchtime in Tokyo.

For swing traders who trade the four-hour and one-hour charts, there are no times not to trade. Whenever you get the signal, you had better be aware of it—24 hours a day and even on or around U.S. holidays (perhaps *especially* around U.S. holidays). As a swing trader, the only time you might pass on a trade would be just ahead of a major economic release, such as central bank interest-rate decisions or the major employment numbers. Swing traders or intermediate-term players also need to be careful on Fridays and in carrying positions over a weekend.

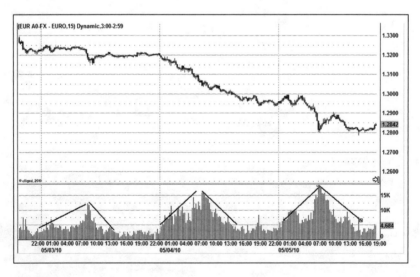

Exhibit 2-2
Source: www.esignal.com.

Fridays have a different character from the rest of the week, because of the implications of there being no retail trading outlets from 5 p.m. Friday EST through 5 p.m. Sunday EST. Over the past few years, Fridays have been known for countertrend moves as traders exit trend trades ahead of the weekends, causing prices to move counter to the predominant trend. For both day traders and swing traders, Friday is often a day to take off because of the undercurrents created by indecision over carrying positions through the weekend by even experienced traders.

Just as there are times of day to avoid trading, for position traders there are also times of the year to either not trade or be very careful trading. Essentially, these are from July 4 through Labor Day (the first weekend in September), and then again for the second half of December through the first week of January, as the markets experience lower trader participation rates and thus low volume during these periods. If you have traded for only a few years or less, you definitely want to avoid trading in these markets because of the choppy price action created by the day-to-day business of institutions and end users in markets where the more experienced traders and speculators are on holiday. Without plenty of experienced traders to provide liquidity in the markets, prices will reverse more quickly and momentum will trump structure, leaving irregular price patterns for inexperienced traders to ponder.

For many experienced traders, late August is a very tough time of the year because traders become restless after the long summer holiday, yet the markets still can't be taken too seriously because of the low volume. Late December should also be avoided, but at least it's only a few weeks, which is much more tolerable from a trader's perspective than the dog days of July and August, which stretch on for weeks and then months. As we said before, either don't trade or be very careful trading. However, you still need to monitor the markets for weekly or monthly trend shifts, which can occur at any time.

Chapter 3

MARKET OVERVIEW

A n overview is a way to categorize a market's price pattern and current trends on all its tradable time frames. It's very important that you make the distinction between the two, as "current trends" is another way of saying short-term trends. While the overview can be used as actionable information, for our preliminary discussions, we are going to consider it as essential reference material. Traders always want to know the price patterns and current trends that are at play in the various markets, along with price structure and momentum, and our overview is going to keep this valuable information updated and available in a spreadsheet that we call our pretrade checklist (see Exhibit 3-1 for an example). This pretrade checklist will also define the type of market we are in (a trending market or a countertrending market), which in turn will determine the trade signals we take and on which time frame we take them. Our goal for this chapter is to teach you how to fill in your pretrade checklist properly.

As we discussed in *Mastering the Currency Market* (McGraw-Hill, 2009), the short-term trend on any chart is equal to the intermediate-term trend on the next lower-time-frame chart and equal to the long-term trend two time frames down. This means that if we know the short-term trend on the monthly chart, we also have the intermediate-term trend on the weekly chart and the long-term trend on the daily chart. It's also much easier to measure the short-term trend on a chart than it would be to measure the intermediate- or long-term trend. Therefore, we are

Pretrade Checklist				
EUR-USD	Calendar	Trend	Pattern	Structure
Monthly		Down	8-year bull, shifted lower 5/2010	50% retrace 2010 sell-off 135.10
Weekly	Light news week	Down	2-1/2 years down	D line 129.22
Daily	9/6 German factory orders 5 a.m.	Up	8-month down / 3-month up	Fib extn 129.49
240-minute		Up	1-month dwn / 1-week up	Bull TL intersect 128.22
60-minute		Down	10-day up	Weekly central pivot 128.06

Exhibit 3-1

interested in knowing only the short-term trend for any time frame, as this gives us the higher-time-frame trends on the lower-time-frame charts. One of our goals for this chapter is to teach you how to determine a market's short-term trend with speed and confidence.

We appreciate the pretrade checklist because by noting and recording the price patterns that are in place and measuring the different trends ourselves, as well as noting the significant structure (that is, support and resistance levels) that is in place on the chart, we draw ourselves in closer to the market, which in turn will start to draw out our intuition. Recording this information in an organized format like this, which we can easily glance at when we're analyzing or trading, is also going to contribute to clear thinking and emphasize the importance of fact-based occurrences and developments in the markets.

Price Pattern

The first thing we need to know about a market before we consider trading it is, what is the current pattern of highs and lows that it is exhibiting? If we are determining this on a daily chart, where each bar or candlestick represents one day, then we want to have at least eight to ten months of data in front of us. We don't need any technical indicators or overlays to help us just yet. The naked eye will do just fine. First we want to see what the pattern is over the course of the entire chart, and then we should focus on any pattern on the right side of the chart. We have three choices to categorize the trends we see: "down," or marked by a clear pattern of lower highs and lower lows; "up," or marked by a clear pattern of higher lows and higher highs; and "sideways," which would be marked by a pattern of highs and lows with no easily discernible direction.

To help us make this determination initially, we can mark the monthly highs and lows with a horizontal line, although with just a bit of experience you will find that the naked eye works just fine. We can also mark the patterns we see with channel lines depending on the symmetry of the price moves for the individual market. Then we would make a directional determination of the overall pattern based on what we see. The chart in Exhibit 3-2 is the daily EUR-USD chart for the first eight months of 2010. We've taken our observations from this chart, specifically that the market was showing a pattern of lower highs and lower lows over an eight-month period, but has shown a pattern of higher lows and higher highs over the last three-month period, and plugged this into our pretrade checklist in Exhibit 3-1. We conduct this same exercise on the different time-frame charts, such as the monthly, the weekly, and down into the intraday charts. Simple observations of what patterns the market is exhibiting are going to help you avoid a lot of distractions and keep you focused on what the market is doing right now, yet still in the context of the overriding pattern.

Exhibit 3-2
Source: www.esignal.com.

The primary reason we want to know what the overriding pattern is, is because markets tend to hold on to these patterns over time. The life of a market move is measured in these patterns, which tend to build slowly over time before accelerating, and then finally ending after traveling further than most analysts and students think they can. As Isaac Newton said, "A body in motion tends to stay in motion," and a market is no different when it comes to following its path of least resistance over time.

We also measure price patterns by drawing parallel trendlines or channel lines. In Exhibit 3-3, we've posted a weekly chart of the stock of G.E. and marked the approximate borders of the price pattern with channel lines. It is these price patterns that put the directional trends into perspective. Smaller directional trends themselves can be seen as the struts or girders of the market, while it is the overall pattern that determines what type of market we are in: a bull market or a bear market. Just as there are times when the direction is down in an uptrend,

Exhibit 3-3
Source: www.esignal.com.

there are times when the direction is up in a downtrend. It's important that you recognize this zigzag pattern and understand that it's
natural that markets often move counter to the overall trend. From a
trader's perspective, we are going to teach you to be aware of both the
current market direction and the overall pattern.

Trendlines

Trendlines are extremely important in our trading for determining the
current trend that is in place, for defining the higher-time-frame
trends, and for providing the chart structure that is so important in our
trade selection. They are also a key determinant in defining the current trend that is in place in a market. The bottom line is, you need
to always update your trendlines. It takes only two high (or low) points
to create a trendline, and updating your trendlines prior to trading
needs to be at the top of your trading plan. Your trading plan will provide the boundaries for your decision-making process, while trendlines

will provide the boundaries for the different markets. Trendlines are key internal structures—support and resistance levels—for all markets. Many times, in reviewing our own trades, we learned that we could avoid losers by keeping our longer-term trendlines updated and not initiating long positions below them or short positions above them, and by heeding the market direction that they highlighted.

In the example of the EUR-USD 15-minute chart shown in Exhibit 3-4, we had a 2-point intermediate-term bear trendline in place above the market and a 2-point short-term bull trendline below the price. The intermediate-term line holds, forcing the price lower, through the short-term trendline, shifting the short-term trend lower and leading to a late afternoon sell-off. This behavior is typical of how price moves and how trendlines can give us an edge in our trading.

One thing to know about drawing trendlines is that there is some subjectivity involved. As a rule, we want to use the last two swing highs

Exhibit 3-4
Source: www.esignal.com.

or lows to draw them from, although any two price points can be used. And we are also going to be drawing trendlines differently for a trending market move and a countertrend move. We cover this in more detail in the chapter on trade setup, but as a rule of thumb, in a trending market, where we are seeing candles of the same color moving in the same direction, we would draw our trendlines off the extremes or wicks of the candles, giving the market room to "breathe," while in a countertrending market, where we are seeing different-colored candles interspersed with no obvious direction, we would go with tighter trendlines drawn from the bodies of the candles, so that we can get into trades more quickly once price breaks back in the direction of the trend. There is nothing wrong with drawing multiple trendlines, either. And you also need to be looking back in time, to the left on the chart, to make sure that previous trendlines are not coming into play. However, at the same time, you do not want to put too much emphasis on previous trendlines if the existing price pattern of highs and lows on the chart is telling you otherwise. While a break of a short-term trendline will often mean a price reaction in the direction of the break, it may not change the overall existing price pattern, which should take precedence over even trendlines.

On the daily GBP-JPY chart in Exhibit 3-5, we see how two-point intermediate-term trend shifts produced sell signals on the leading indicator 14-3-3 stochastic in the lowest panel on the chart. It's important to remember that in technical analysis, price must move first, before the technical indicators can record a shift in momentum. What the technical indicators are good for, however, is confirming price action. Most experienced traders look at the angle of price on the chart to gauge a market's speed, or momentum, while most analysts look to the technical indicators for this information. It is always best that you look to price first for the information that you need, and use the technical indicators to confirm. In this example, we see the relative effectiveness of using a combination of a trendline break on a closing basis

Exhibit 3-5
Source: www.esignal.com.

and a stochastic cross for a trigger. This simple, basic signal, which we taught in *Mastering the Currency Market*, provides an effective trigger because it combines a price pattern (the break of a trendline on a closing basis) and a leading indicator (the stochastic).

A drawback of technical indicators in general, and oscillators such as a stochastic in particular, is that they are designed to roll back and forth, recording all momentum shifts that occur, with no distinction between impulse price action (think trending markets) and reactive price action (think corrective price action). In addition, a drawback of trendlines is that when price goes sideways, or corrects, the linear trendline gives the appearance of having been broken when price is just pausing before a resumption of the overall move. This problem has often troubled analysts and has led many to opt for moving averages in an attempt to find a more fluid boundary to contain price and help identify direction.

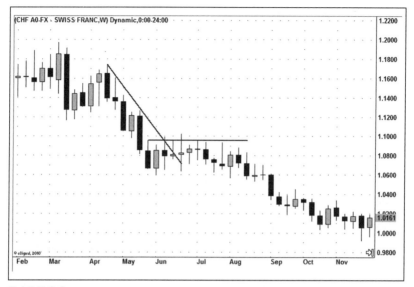

Exhibit 3-6
Source: www.esignal.com.

Our solution for determining that a trend is still in place despite a trendline breach in a sideways market is what we call a directional line. A directional line is essentially the horizontal line created by the high of the lowest closing candle in a downtrend or the low of the highest closing candle in an uptrend. We can draw our directional lines on any time frame. On the daily chart in Exhibit 3-6, we see price moving beyond the bear trendline by virtue of moving sideways, but remaining below the high of the lowest closing candle, our daily directional line. Not only do directional lines help us in determining a market's current direction, but they also provide chart structure (support and resistance), particularly when they converge with pivot points and retracement levels. Often intraday swing highs and lows are posted on the lower-time-frame directional lines, or become directional lines as price and time move forward. We use trendlines combined with directional lines to determine a market's current, or short-term, trend.

Directional Lines

We originally designed directional lines to help the trader determine whether a signal or trigger is a trend trade (that is, one that is going in the same direction as the higher-time-frame trends) or a countertrend trade (one that is going against the next higher-time-frame trend). Directional lines are an excellent tool for keeping track of the trends on the different time frames without having to keep switching back and forth between charts, and they mark what we call a change of direction. Again, the directional line marks the low of the current highest closing candle in an uptrend or the high of the current lowest closing candle in a downtrend, and it extends out to the right side of the chart on whichever time frame we need to measure or see.

The side of the directional line that price is on helps to define the current direction. In most simplistic terms, we can say that if price is below the line, the trend is lower; if price is above the line, the trend is higher (see Exhibit 3-7). We can place the appropriate line on the monthly chart, then drop down to the weekly chart and place the appropriate line

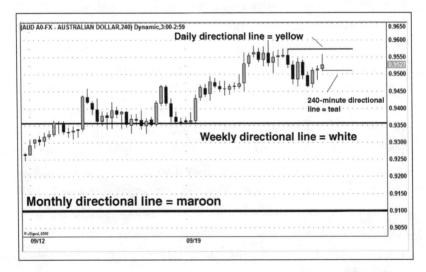

Exhibit 3-7
Source: www.esignal.com.

there, then drop down to the daily chart, and so on. The line does not move until we get a new high closing candle or a new low closing candle in the same direction, in which case the line switches to the new high closing or low closing candle, or until price reverses and closes beyond the line, in which case the line switches again to mark a new high or low closing candle in the new direction. When a candle does close beyond the line to reverse direction, we call this occurrence a change of direction, and the candle that shifts the line is called a change-of-direction candle. There can be only one directional line per time frame.

By learning to draw these directional lines ourselves, we will be able to glance at one chart and see the current trends on the higher time frames. This will help us in keeping track of the current trends on the different time frames. Once you have worked with the lines for a bit, you will see that they keep us more settled in our analysis. In trading, it's very important to maintain a relaxed, yet focused state. The more we are switching back and forth between time frames, the less we are keeping our focus. The lines allow us to focus more on price developments on the right side of the chart because we can see with just a glance how price is behaving relative to its higher-time-frame trends. Having this important aspect of price direction calculated for us in a simple, visual manner, combined with trendlines, helps to draw our intuition into the trading process.

To keep track of our directional lines, we color-code them, making it easier to identify which line corresponds with which time frame. For the sake of this book, however, we've gone with black-and-white lines in our figures. Jay Norris uses a light grey color for the background on his trading screens, which has the added benefit of being easier on your eyes, particularly if you spend a good deal of time looking at computer screens. Here are the color codes for the directional lines:

Maroon = monthly
White = weekly

Yellow = daily
Teal = 240-minute
Pink = 60-minute

The primary use of the directional lines is to help measure current trends in a market so that we know when we have a change of direction. If by definition we can define the current direction of the trend in any market on any time frame, then we must also know at what point that market changed direction. If I'm telling you that the trend is definitively up, then I must be able to tell you at what point it changed from down to up. The directional line is the specific level on the chart that identifies the point in price and time when a market changed direction— that's past tense—which is impressive because it means that you can go back in time and back-test what we're telling you. But what's really impressive about this is that the directional line by definition will also give us that future point in price that a market will have to eclipse to change direction. These levels frequently become pivotal areas on the chart, often providing support or resistance. Their strength, however, lies not in price bouncing off them or consolidating around them, but in its closing beyond them. What is essential for you to understand about them is how they move. The line can move only under two conditions: price closes beyond it and we get a change of direction, which is why we call the candle that breaches the line on a closing basis a change-of-direction candle, or we get a new high or low closing candle in the same direction as the trend, and the line continues up or down along with the current trend. Take a moment now to open up your chart package, pull up a daily chart of any market you are interested in trading in, and print it out. Go ahead and mark the low of the highest closing candle in the most recent rally on the chart, and then mark the high of the lowest closing candle in the most recent downtrend. Perhaps the most recent candle is the one you marked. Keep the chart handy because you will need it following the next section.

Determining Market Direction

The most important thing we can teach you is how to determine a market's current direction. And if we can teach you how to determine this on one time frame, we can teach it to you on all time frames. And as we said before when defining our directional lines, if we can tell you whether a trend is up or down, then we must also be able to tell you at what point in both price and time the trend shifted, recording a change of direction. That point is determined by the combination of a trend-line break and a directional-line shift, both on a closing basis. We make this determination for the various time frames of the markets we are interested in trading, and we record it in our pretrade checklist.

We need only two points on the chart to draw a trendline, which means that it takes only two candles to make a trend. Therefore, if we update our trendlines continuously, we will see right away when a candle breaches the previous short-term trendline and then closes beyond it. If it can fulfill this condition, and also close beyond the directional line, then this is by definition a trend shift. While one candle doesn't make a trend, one candle can certainly shift a trend. The next time you are looking at a chart, you need to find those points in both price and time where a market fulfilled these two criteria and recorded a short-term trend shift. In Exhibit 3-8 we've marked the short-term trend shifts that this technique recorded on a weekly EUR-USD chart.

The technique of using trendline/directional-line shifts to measure the short-term trend changes in a market generally works well on the higher-time-frame charts of those markets that are actively traded, with the EUR-USD being a good example. Generally speaking, the lower down the time frames we go, the more complex market movement becomes, which is what contributes heavily to the high failure rate of traders, particularly those who try to trade the lower time frames without proper training. Using this technique, however, helps us to highlight short-term trend shifts on any time frame. In Exhibit 3-9, the short-term trend shifts on a four-hour GBP-USD chart are highlighted.

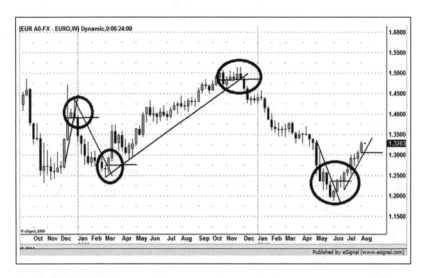

Exhibit 3-8
Source: www.esignal.com.

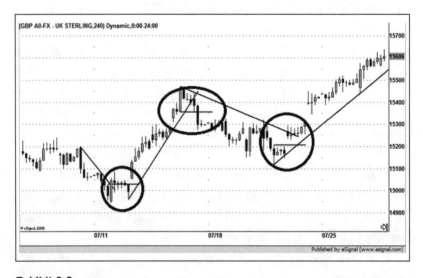

Exhibit 3-9
Source: www.esignal.com.

It's important to always remember that trading is an art, and that drawing trendlines can be subjective, which points out the importance of keeping track of the pattern of unfolding highs and lows, and experience. The directional line, however, is not subjective. It is always going to be the same every time. You will find that the directional line's being static will help you in your selection of which trendlines to draw, and in keeping you patient. And it will certainly help you to stay on top of which direction a stock, currency, or commodity is currently pointed in, which is what it was designed for.

Now take out the chart that we instructed you to print out at the end of the previous section, where you drew in the directional lines. Now draw in your trendlines. Based on your directional lines and the trendlines, you should be starting to see the current direction for that market (chart). You need to practice determining the short-term trend in the various markets using this technique, and plugging that directional bias into a spreadsheet (pretrade checklist) of your own. You should already be starting to see how effective this combination of trendline shift and directional-line shift can be.

Exhibit 3-10 demonstrates how the directional line moves. Every time the GBP-USD posts a higher closing candle, the directional line, which marks the low of that highest closing candle, is adjusted higher.

Trending and Countertrending Markets

A trending market is defined as one in which the current trend is moving in the same direction as the higher-time-frame trends, while a countertrending market is one in which the current trend is counter to the higher-time-frame trends. An example of a trending market would be if we are trading an hourly chart, and that trend is higher, and the four-hour trend and the daily trend are also higher. Similarly, a countertrending market would be one in which we are trading a

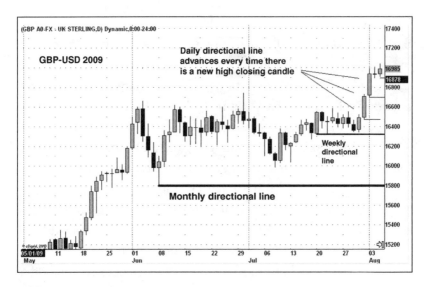

Exhibit 3-10
Source: www.esignal.com.

four-hour chart where the trend is lower, yet the daily and weekly trends are higher. It is important for us as traders to be able to distinguish between a trend trade and a countertrend trade because this information will affect how quickly and on what time frame we get into and out of trades, or if we will even trade at all. As a rule of thumb, if a trigger is a countertrend trade, we will get into it more quickly and look to exit more quickly as well to protect ourselves, so we would use shorter-term charts where our risk would be smaller, because our decision making would be based on shorter time horizon candles. By definition, countertrend, or reactive, price moves are much shorter lived than trending, or impulsive, price moves.

When we are first learning to trade, we should decide ahead of time to pass on taking countertrend trades because of the higher risk and lower reward associated with them, or we should take countertrend trades only in a demo account. When we are trend trading, we will be using higher-time-frame charts and looser stops. Exhibit 3-11 is an

Exhibit 3-11
Source: www.esignal.com.

example of a trending market. Based on the directional lines on the chart, it's very clear which way we should have been leaning in early September 2010. Given that the monthly, weekly, and daily charts are all coordinated and pointing higher, it's no surprise that the market gave us a powerful rally.

With the directional lines in place on this 15-minute intraday chart of AUD-USD from September of 2010, you can see the advantages of trend trading in a market where the higher time frames are aligned. In fact, for trend traders, the best times to trade are when the higher time frames are coordinated because you are going to enjoy the most favorable risk/reward scenario on your trades. We see time after time on this chart how the lows provided support and price continued to post higher lows and higher highs. If there is a science that can describe price movement, it would be fractal geometry, where what occurs on the higher time frames is replicated on the lower time frames, but with a slight degree of complexity. When you are in a market in which the higher time frames are coordinated, it's important that you also be mindful of waiting for the intraday time frames to be coordinated. Often people who are learning to trade will analyze the direction of the higher-time-frame charts, such as the daily chart, correctly and determine to take intraday signals in the same direction as the daily. There is nothing wrong with this thinking, but you will still need to be mindful of which time frame you are going to be taking the signal on, and of the market's stance on the next higher time frames.

If you decided to take a signal on the 15-minute chart, you would still need to be mindful of the trends on the 60-minute and 240-minute charts, which equate to the intermediate- and long-term trends for that market, and make sure that these trends were not working against you. For example, you would not take a buy trigger on a 15-minute chart if the trend on the 60-minute chart is lower with increasing bearish momentum. Likewise, you would not take a buy signal on the 15-minute chart if the 240-minute candle had just closed below significant support and was showing bearish momentum. Making observations like these ahead of time, and using common sense and patience, will go a long way in improving your trade selection and avoiding losing trades.

As a rule of thumb, in a trending market, we want to wait for higher-time-frame confirmation, meaning that we want to see that price pattern, structure, and momentum on the higher-time-frame charts are aligned with the signal on the lower-time-frame chart. It's important to understand that in a trending market, direction is dictated by the higher time frames. If you take a trade signal and the direction on the next higher time frame is not in agreement, this would be considered a countertrend trade. For a trade to be designated a "trend trade," you need either the next higher-time-frame chart (the intermediate-term trend) or the long-term time-frame chart to be moving in the same direction as the trade signal you are considering.

An exception to this rule would be if a trade signal is counter to the intermediate-term trend and the longer-term time frame is questionable,

Exhibit 3-12
Source: www.esignal.com.

but price is finding support or resistance on a significant retracement level such as a 0.618, or 66 percent of that long-term trend. We can consider this a trend trade signal, and because it is occurring on significant structure, our risk on the trade is defined. For further information on retracements and their interpretation and Fibonacci levels see *Mastering the Currency Market*.

In Exhibit 3-12, we have an example of a market in which the trend on the daily chart is counter to the trend on the weekly chart. When we see that we are in a market in which the daily and weekly trends are pointed in different directions, we can expect choppy trading. We call these "countertrending" markets because the trend on the daily chart is counter to the trend on the weekly. In a countertrend market such as this, direction will be dictated by the lower time frames.

The intraday chart in Exhibit 3-13 shows us in more detail how in a countertrend environment, we will see instances in which neither support nor resistance holds, and in which markets are stopping and turning much more quickly. Price patterns and market behavior can

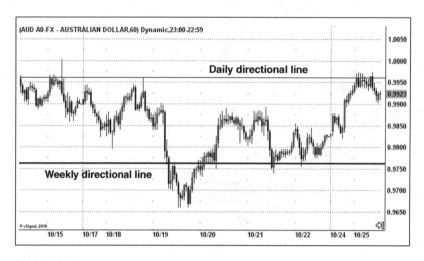

Exhibit 3-13
Source: www.esignal.com.

appear to be much less predictable than in markets in which the higher time frames are coordinated. In such a market, the trader will be better served by trading lower time frames and not waiting for higher-time-frame coordination. In the section on trade triggers, we will cover this again, and further define countertrend triggers.

Whether the market is trending or countertrending is an important distinction to make, and one that will definitely dictate which time frame you need to be trading on. Exhibit 3-14 shows a 60-minute chart of EUR-JPY where the market is above the weekly directional line and below the monthly directional line. Choppy, directionless trading ensues, with the market being hesitant to move too far from the weekly line. The lesson here is that you will find trading to be less time-consuming and more rewarding if you stick to trading markets in which the monthly and weekly or the weekly and daily time frames are coordinated. Likewise, unless you have the proper training and mindset, you should avoid trading in markets in which the higher time frames are in flux, such as the last two examples.

Exhibit 3-14
Source: www.esignal.com.

Countertrending markets can be defined as markets in which the lower-time-frame trend is *counter* to the higher-time-frame trend— there is a divergence between the two trends, such as between the monthly and weekly trends on this chart. Another distinction to make is that in a countertrending market, we would use trendlines drawn from the bodies of the candles so that we can record the turns more quickly, whereas in a trending market, we would draw our trendlines from wick to wick to give the market, and our stops, more room.

Directional Trading and Higher-Time-Frame Confirmation

Directional trading, also known as discretionary trading, is what most retail traders strive to succeed at. In this type of trading, the traders attempt to figure out the market's current direction and either position themselves in that direction at the most opportune time or wait until the market changes direction and position themselves to be able to profit from a continuation of this new direction. Contrary to what most beginning traders think, most traders who work for investment banks or proprietary trading shops are not directional traders. Many of the traders employed by investment banks and prop shops are essentially mechanics who are trained in the use of countertrending methods, continuously scanning markets in search of those times when one market price gets slightly out of line with a related market—that's when they position their firm's money in those markets so that they profit when price snaps back into line. These traders' method is called arbitrage, and if they can borrow money at 2.6 percent and make 5 or 6 percent in their trading operations, they are very profitable.

The big investment houses in London and New York also employ traders called market makers. This is the trading category that most professional traders fall into today. In many ways, they aren't traders at all by most old-school traders' definition. They are computer programmers who write and service the programs that investment firms and trading boutiques use in an attempt to take the other side of every trade that you and I make. When you read stories saying that the investment bank Golden Stash made money every day of the previous quarter, it does not mean that Golden Stash has learned the secret of how to pick and train traders, it means that Golden Stash's market-making operations managed to book, or get on the other side of, a lot of trades and then offset those trades at a sliver of a profit.

Big investment banks and prop trading shops aren't interested in directional trading because it does not make sense from an odds-maker's perspective. The average directional trader places the odds against herself every time she buys or sells at the market. The minute she hits the button to enter a trade by buying the offer or selling the bid, she gives up an edge. Professional market makers or arbitrage traders try to never give up the edge of buying on the bid and selling on the offer. They are not in business to predict where a market is going to move to next; they are in the business of buying the bid and selling the offer, and they want their computers to do that for them thousands of times a day in hundreds of markets.

We, on the other hand, are not interested in that fractional edge. We would much rather play the opposite of that game and trade only once a day, but position ourselves in a market that trends in our direction all day, or for two or three days, or for two or three months. The way we attempt do this is by trading in the same direction as the higher-time-frame trends and recognizing when those trends are shifting. Knowing how to use higher-time-frame charts to confirm a price signal on a lower-time-frame chart is an essential skill for directional traders, and one that can reward you greatly once you master it. Many students will become impatient and take a trade that is coordinated on the lower time frames, but not on the higher time frames. This is a mistake and is often a waste of time, energy, and, more important, money.

While you may not always have all the time frames line up, there will be times when this happens. More often than not, though, if you are trading an intraday chart and you have the current trend on the daily chart lined up in the same direction, you are going to have the wind at your back. If you have the knowledge to identify markets where the intraday trends are moving in the same direction as the daily and weekly trends, then you are going to put yourself in a position to reap the trader's reward.

Here are the time frames we analyze and trade from:

Monthly ⟷ Weekly ⟷ Daily ⟷
240 min ⟷ 60 min ⟷ 15 min ⟷ 3 min

The different time frames we use must remain four to six increments apart to maintain continuity.

Monthly/4 = weekly chart
Weekly/5 = daily chart
Daily/6 = 240-minute chart
240/4 = 60-minute chart
60/4 = 15-minute chart
15/5 = 3-minute chart

When analyzing a market, it's important to know what price direction is on the next two higher time frames. If we are trading off a 60-minute chart, we would look to our 240-minute and daily charts for confirmation. This is important in order to keep continuity, but it's also important because by doing so, you will always be aware of what is going on in the short-, intermediate-, and long-term trends. When we are trading a 60-minute chart, we want to view the current trend on the 60-minute chart as the short-term trend, the current trend on the 240-minute chart as the intermediate-term trend, and the current trend on the daily chart as the long-term trend. Likewise, if we see a signal on the daily chart, we look to the trend on the weekly and monthly charts for confirmation. If we see a signal or setup on the 15-minute chart, we look to the 60-minute and 240-minute charts for confirmation.

The way we use these higher time frames is identical to the way we taught you to identify direction on just one time frame earlier in this chapter. And then we take only trade signals that are in the direction of the trend(s) on the higher time frames. If market volatility is high—that is, if the rate of price change is increasing—we would focus on having the signal on the short-term trend be in line with the intermediate-term trend; and if the volatility is modest, then we would favor signals that are in line with the long-term trend. Exhibits 3-12, 3-13, and 3-14 provide good examples of how to use the higher time frames to assist in taking a directional trade on the lower time frames.

(AUD A0-FX - AUSTRALIAN DOLLAR,240) Dynamic,3:00-2:59

AUD-USD 4-Hour Chart

8/9/10 7:00 a.m. through 11:00 a.m.
Change-of-direction candle circled

Exhibit 3-15
Source: www.esignal.com.

In Exhibit 3-15 we have a change of direction, as noted by the directional line penetration on a closing basis, and we have price closing below the trendline, which means that the trend has shifted from up to down. At this point, we can call the short-term trend on the 240-minute chart lower, and we would record this in our pretrade checklist spreadsheet. We then drop down to the next lower-time-frame chart (see Exhibit 3-16), the 60-minute chart, and update our directional line and trendline on this time frame.

In Exhibit 3-16, we have both the current 240-minute trend lower and the current 60-minute trend lower. We would also record this in our checklist spreadsheet, and know that it tells us that this would be potentially an ideal time to take a sell signal on the 15-minute chart, because both the intermediate- and long-term trends are already pointed lower for this time frame. Also, as we can see in Exhibit 3-17 on the 15-minute chart of AUD-USD for this same day, the next sell signal on the 15-minute chart does indeed prove to have been a winning trade if managed properly.

Exhibit 3-16
Source: www.esignal.com.

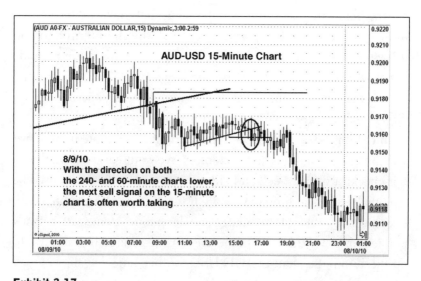

Exhibit 3-17
Source: www.esignal.com.

Notice how we went with a body-to-body trendline to cover the short-term trend on this 15-minute chart? This is because the market was showing no real directional bias other than sideways, and with its intermediate- and long-term trends already lower, we opt for the tighter trendline that the body-to-body line gives us so that we can get into the trade more quickly once the higher time frames assert themselves. You will see in your own studies and back-tests how effective taking signals in the same direction as the longer-term trends is, and how ineffective taking signals against, or counter to, the longer-term trends is.

Divergence between Time Frames

When talking about countertrend price movement, it's appropriate to talk about divergence. There are two types of divergence for us. First, there is divergence between the directions of price on two different time frames, for example, the direction on the monthly chart is higher, but the direction on the weekly chart is lower, such as in AUD-USD on the left side of Exhibit 3-18. And then there is the second kind of divergence, which is divergence between price and momentum in a single time frame. When we refer to divergence, more often than not we are referring to the second type of divergence, which is that between price and momentum. For this section, however, we are referring to divergence between the trends on different time frames.

To determine and collate the direction of the current trend on the various markets you follow, you'll be able to glance at your pretrade checklist, where you'll see whether a market is trending or countertrending on its different time frames. If the monthly, weekly, and daily charts are all pointed in the same direction, then this market is trending on its higher time frames. If the 240-minute, 60-minute, and 15-minute trends are all moving in the same direction, then the market is trending on its lower time frames. On the other hand, if the higher time frames are in flux—that is, they are currently moving in different

AUD-USD	Short-Term Trend	EUR-USD	Short-Term Trend
Monthly	Up	Monthly	Down
Weekly	Down	Weekly	Down
Daily	Up	Daily	Down
240-minute	Up	240-minute	Down
60-minute	Down	60-minute	Up
15-minute	Down	15-minute	Up

Exhibit 3-18

directions—then we say that the market is experiencing countertrending behavior. Likewise, if the 240-minute trend is up but the 60-minute trend is down, as in Exhibit 3-18, then we have countertrending conditions on the intraday charts. Again we make these important determinations by using both trendlines and directional lines.

Price Structure and Pivot Points

Support and resistance levels are the internal structure of a market. In its simplest form, trading can be described as the pattern created by price movement—momentum—reacting to structure. As important as trendlines are, and to a lesser degree directional lines, pivot points are, in our estimation, the most important structure on the intraday charts, even more important than retracements. Pivot points provide the most targeted areas on the chart for professionals to exit their shorter-term trades, or to initiate new trades, once price closes beyond a pivot in the direction of the current price pattern. Whether it be the monthly pivots, the weekly pivots, or the daily pivots, these influential areas on the chart act like magnets for price action. The key is that you use the floor pivots, which do not include the opening price in the equation, and that for the daily pivots, you use the 5 p.m. EDT closing price, which ensures that you will be using the proper high, low, and closing prices for the equation. The correct equation is

$$\text{Central pivot (P)} = (H + L + C)/3$$
$$\text{Resistance (R1)} = (2 \times P) - L$$
$$R2 = P + H - L$$
$$\text{Support (S1)} = (2 \times P) - H$$
$$S2 = P - H + L$$

Notice that the only inputs are the market's high price (H), its low price (L), and its closing price (C) for a given time period. The numbers used to calculate the pivot points are derived from price only, making them fact-based levels. And as with so many tools in trading, the use of the pivots is straightforward. Once price closes above the central pivot, and the current price pattern is one of higher lows and higher highs, it becomes more likely that price will rise to R1, and if it closes above R1, it becomes more likely that it will migrate toward R2. Likewise, if price closes below the central pivot and is exhibiting a pattern of lower highs and lower lows, it becomes more likely that price will fall to S1, and if it closes below S1, it becomes more likely that it will continue toward S2. The different pivot levels are good areas on the chart at which to gauge a market's strength or weakness by monitoring price behavior.

A series of indecisive candles—candles with small real bodies—that give the chart the appearance of being "spiky" and occur at an extreme such as S2 or R2 would hint at a potential market correction, or even a reversal. The same type of candles occurring around the central pivot might favor consolidation, and we would probably be more attuned for a continuation in the same direction that price was moving in before it was showing indecision. We can also use the pivots to confirm price direction. For example, if a market is showing us a pattern of lower highs and lower lows and is trading below its central pivot, we would take this as a confirmation of market weakness. Likewise, if we see a pattern of higher lows and higher highs, this would confirm strength. And for those times when price seems out of sorts with its pivot points— for example, the market is in an uptrend, but it is well below its central pivot—we would understand that it is likely to be counter-trending, and we would know to avoid trading that market that day.

We would also look for areas where we had a confluence of structure, such as a previous daily high or low, trendline, or retracement level in the same area on the chart as the pivot point and be aware of price activity at this level for setups and potential signals in line with the existing price pattern. Above all, we need to look for structure to complement the price pattern. And it is at those times when we see setups and signals with the pivots fitting the price pattern perfectly that we would expect the largest price moves.

Science tells us that when a species's needs are aligned with its environment, that species will grow. What you need to understand is that the same concept applies to traders. As a trader, your day-to-day environment is whatever stock, commodity, or currency you wish to trade, while your overall environment is the business cycle, or what a technical analyst might call the "wave count." Just as any life form relies on environmental conditions for survival first, you need to learn to put market conditions first, and never forget that your needs and the market's needs must first be aligned for you to survive, and they must remain aligned if you are to thrive. And just as important, your "wants" are nonexistent from your environment's perspective.

So the overall environment is the business cycle, or market price pattern, while the immediate environment is the individual market(s) you trade. We can break that individual market down into its overriding framework, the business cycle or wave count, which will be reflected in the price pattern of highs and lows on the chart, and its internal structure, which is its support and resistance levels. By waiting for the internal structure to complement the price pattern, we are increasing our odds of success because we are aligning our trading with the market's environmental conditions. It's important to realize that even when the trends and structure are aligned and showing momentum, we still don't know what will happen. From a psychological standpoint, you need to realize that you do not know what the market will do next, but by executing your trading plan, you will go along with where the market goes. As a student of the markets, it is your job to go back in time on your charts and find those signals where structure—pivots, trendlines, retracements, and so on—complemented the price pattern so that you can see the price action that followed.

In Exhibit 3-19, we get a good example of structure complementing price pattern. We have an existing uptrend in place, with a long-term trendline marking the bottom. On the left side of the chart, we can see that price is struggling to hold above its central pivot—this is a case in which chart structure is not lined up with price pattern, and we see sloppy, directionless trade. Once price clears the central pivot and then consolidates above it, the market is in a much better position to advance. Also notice that from 8/1 through 8/2 we see a very subtle pattern of higher lows. With chart structure complementing both the long-term and current price patterns, the next buy signal

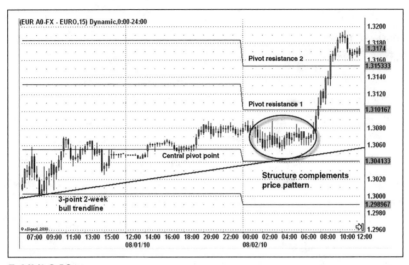

Exhibit 3-19
Source: www.esignal.com.

turns out to be an especially generous one. What's particularly inter-esting about this example is that there were no significant economic releases or news events on the calendar prior to the sharp rally between 7 a.m. and 8 a.m. on 8/2/10.

Pivot points and weekly and monthly highs and lows, in our esti-mation, are as significant as trendlines. What makes pivot points so critical is that they are horizontal, and each individual pivot can provide support or resistance. As with trendlines, when price closes beyond one pivot, it becomes likely that it will migrate to the next pivot. But trendlines can work only one way in that regard, and they are not as scalable as pivots. There are also specific pivots for different time frames, something that you will come to appreciate if you are both a position trader and a day trader. And probably the most impor-tant aspect of using pivot points in your trading is that they will help you to recognize both sides of the market. If price closes above the pivot, you are looking to be a buyer, and if price closes below the pivot, you are looking to be a seller.

Retracements to Assist in Positioning

Both an advantage and a drawback of the pretrade checklist is that it gives the analyst or trader a way to definitively identify trend and take his opinion out of the process. This is an advantage for those traders who are in the earlier stages of learning to trade, but it can be a hindrance to the experienced trader's intuition. Very often a market will retrace an impulse move, and the experienced trader will recognize what is happening based on price momentum and candlestick behavior. If he waits for higher-time-frame confirmation as measured by the pretrade checklist, however, he may not get the most favorable trade placement that a signal on the lower-time-frame chart will offer. The short-term trend on a higher-time-frame chart can still be pointing down even though the market is experiencing a correction, or a reactive move, following a larger impulse up move. If we waited for higher-time-frame confirmation using the pretrade checklist definition, we would miss the opportunity to take the first buy trigger on that lower time frame following the correction.

Under these circumstances, a retracement level such as 0.382, 50 percent, or 0.618 will provide support or resistance that the price will use to mount a setup and trigger on the lower time frame. If the setup occurs on an obvious retracement level, and is a potential higher low or lower high on the higher-time-frame chart, we can use this in lieu of higher-time-frame confirmation.

In Exhibit 3-20, we see a trendline and a directional-line break on a closing basis provide a buy signal on a daily chart. Earlier in the chapter, we stated that in the case of price finding support (or resistance) on an intermediate- or long-term trendline or on a significant retracement level of the previous higher-time-frame move, we can consider this to be higher-time-frame confirmation. In this example, because price held the 0.618 retracement level of the previous higher-time-frame up move, essentially recording a higher low on the longer-term charts, we can take this as higher-time-frame confirmation.

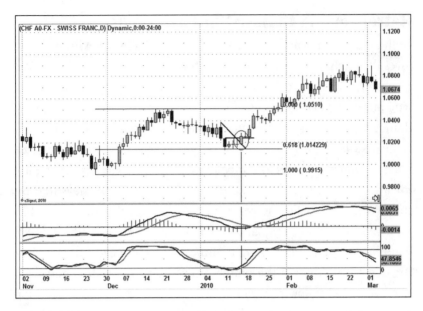

Exhibit 3-20
Source: www.esignal.com.

Arguably it can also be called a countertrend trade on the daily chart, but we can see from the weekly chart in Exhibit 3-21 that the sell-off in late December through mid-January was a correction of the impulse up move that started in early December.

The ideal trade setup for most experienced traders is taking a countertrend signal on the short-term chart that is in line with the dominant trend on the long-term chart. By giving the trader the freedom to take a signal on the lower-time-frame chart based on support or resistance on the higher-time-frame chart, it keeps guidelines in place in your trading plan, but still gives more experienced traders room for their intuition and the opportunity to get better positioning in the market. We can also use the strength or weakness of a market move in deciding which retracement levels to monitor. If we see a strong move, we would want to monitor the 0.382 and 50 percent retracement levels, while a slower rally would mean that we would monitor the 50 percent

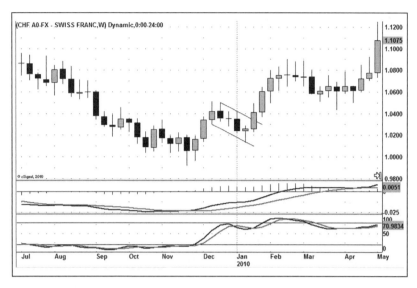

Exhibit 3-21
Source: www.esignal.com.

and 0.618 retracement levels. When we see a retracement go beyond 66 percent, it generally opens the door to a 100 percent retracement, which is how sideways formations or rectangles occur. These are also called "boxes," as price will oscillate back and forth in a rectangle box as it consolidates the previous move. Often the bottoms or tops of these boxes are found at a confluence of a significant retracement level from a monthly or even yearly chart and a higher-time-frame pivot point or historical swing high or low.

Knowing that markets have a penchant for somewhat predictable retracements, also known as corrections, will help us in managing trades. As much as we'd like the price to accelerate our way in a trade, it is much more common for price to extend a move for two or three candles in our direction, then pause and retreat, or retrace. Despite these retracements being commonplace (expectable, really), many traders still give in to their emotions and exit trades prematurely right at the end of a retracement because they can't take the pain of the lower-time-frame direction moving against them so far. Often enough, this occurs just before price recovers as the higher-time-frame structure holds and the longer-term trend resumes.

Once you understand that retracements are a function of price discovery, that they have to occur, or there would be no need for a market, you become better prepared to weather them in your trading, or even take advantage of them. We would do this by marking the common Fibonacci levels, such as 50 percent and 0.618, and monitoring these levels for buy or sell setups following a retracement to these levels, to position ourselves in the same direction as the long-term trend. Should the previous move reassert itself, we would have favorable positioning and might expect the market to move on to eclipse the previous swing high or low. If not, we can assume a reasonable risk such as just beyond a 66 percent retracement, and stop ourselves out of the trade there. The bottom line is that "expect retracements" is good advice.

Chapter 4

IDENTIFYING STRENGTH
AND WEAKNESS

I dentifying strength and weakness is a simple, effective concept that will help you to determine which markets to take which signals in. The most important thing to remember is that you want to be buying strength and selling weakness; that is, you want to take buy signals in the strong markets and sell signals in the weak markets. The easiest way to look at strength and weakness measurements on the short-term chart is by looking to the quote board on our charting package or trading platform, which gives us the various markets' net change reading for that day.

In Exhibit 4-1, we see three of the major currencies on the upper left of the quote board. We can see that the AUD-USD is down 60 pips, the EUR-USD is down 107 pips, and the GBP-USD is up 110 pips. What this means is that if these pairs were giving buy signals, we would focus on the GBP-USD because it is the strongest. Likewise, if these pairs were to roll lower, we would focus on sell signals in the EUR-USD because it is the weakest of the three. Very often currency pairs roll up and roll down at the same time, and even experienced traders aren't sure which market to go long or short when they do. You will find that this simple observation of measuring a market's daily or weekly net change to determine strength or weakness relative to the other

AUD AO-FX		EUR AO-FX		GBP AO-FX		NZD AO-FX		CHF AO-FX	
O	0.9901	O	1.3954	O	15727	O	0.7518	O	0.9711
H	0.9930	H	1.3982	H	15896	H	0.7543	H	0.9882
L	0.9815	L	1.3826	L	15691	L	0.7472	L	0.9704
C	0.9841	C	1.3847	C	15837	C	0.7486	C	0.9854
%	-0.61%	%	-0.77%	%	+0.70%	%	-0.43%	%	+1.47%
▲	▼-0.0060	▲	▼-0.0107	▲	▲110	▲	▼-0.0032	▲	▲0.0143

AUDJPY AO-FX		CADJPY AO-FX		EURJPY AO-FX		GBPJPY AO-FX		JPY AO-FX	
O	79.97	O	79.197	O	112.73	O	127.05	O	80.78
H	80.35	H	79.619	H	113.28	H	129.15	H	81.65
L	79.89	L	79.141	L	112.42	L	126.84	L	80.60
C	80.17	C	79.570	C	112.82	C	129.00	C	81.45
%	+0.25%	%	+0.47%	%	+0.08%	%	+1.53%	%	+0.83%
▲	▲0.20	▲	▲0.373	▲	▲0.09	▲	▲1.95	▲	▲0.67

ZG Z0		ZC #F		ZW #F		ZN Z0		ZB Z0	
O	13390	O	5670	O	6740	O	126100	O	13131
H	13436	H	5772	H	6990	H	126140	H	13207
L	13283	L	5620	L	6704	L	125200	L	13017
C	13391	C	5710	C	6920	C	125225	C	13019
%	+0.02%	%	+0.40%	%	+2.67%	%	-0.57%	%	-1.16%
▲	▲3	▲	▲22	▲	▲180	▲	▼-230	▲	▼-117

Exhibit 4-1
Source: www.esignal.com.

currencies, and taking buy signals in the strong pairs when they roll up and sell signals in the weak pairs when they roll down, can make a marked difference in your trading. Buying strength and selling weakness is a tenet of trading for sure, and this powerful tactic shows you exactly how to do that. It will prove particularly beneficial if you trade intraday.

In the intraday trading plans we provide for our clients, one of the first things we highlight is "take strength and weakness reading," and this is a simple, effective way to do that. From a psychological standpoint, you have to be aware of the pull to buy weakness because you perceive value, or to sell strength because you believe that something is overpriced. In trading, this logic will get you into trouble. Markets have a powerful tendency to overshoot even the most aggressive targets because of the tendency of inexperienced traders to do exactly the wrong thing in this regard, selling when they perceive price is overbought, then being forced themselves to pay even higher prices the next day or next week as fear and the margin department prompt them to cover their positions to avoid further losses.

By noting which pairs are stronger and which pairs are weaker several times a day as the markets roll from the Asian session to the European session to the U.S. session, you will develop a feel for which pairs are leaders and which pairs are laggards, and this can help your trade selection when you are deciding which pairs to trade. Often the various pairs will give trade signals at the same approximate time, and you may not be well capitalized enough to take them all. Or you may have a good feel for which pair is the lead horse and which one is pulling up short. Either way, you will have a solid clue as to which market to deploy your trading capital in for maximum benefit. In our live trading exercises, we use this tactic often in determining which market(s) to focus on.

Momentum Oscillators

An oscillator is a technical indicator that uses data derived from the components of a market's price range, generally taking an average of those variables over a specific time period, so that the tool oscillates up and down, allowing us to take a measure of a market's underlying momentum. Momentum is certainly worth noting in our overview and recording in our pretrade checklist. The primary oscillator we use for conducting our market overview is the moving average convergence/divergence, or MACD. The MACD is a versatile indicator that combines a trend-following function with a centered oscillator, also known as a momentum indicator. By developing MACD, a derivative of moving averages, Gerald Appel gave us a hybrid tool that both is helpful in determining the market's present direction and measures momentum (the rate of change of price over time). We defined the different components of the indicator in *Mastering the Currency Market* (McGraw-Hill, 2009), so there is no need to go into details of the indicator's construction. The typical variables for the MACD ratio are "12, 26, 9," which we will use for our examples.

What you really need to know about oscillators is they are generally derived from two moving averages—in our examples, a MACD using the 12-bar and 26-bar exponential moving averages (EMAs) are used—and a moving average of the difference between those first two averages, which is plotted along the center line to create a histogram. The 12-bar exponential moving average is the MACD, the 26-bar exponential moving average is the trigger line, and the histogram is calculated from a 9-bar moving average of the difference between the 12- and 26-bar EMAs. The difference between the MACD and its trigger line—either moving toward each other or moving away from each other—indicates both direction and momentum, and can have predictive value.

As the moving averages approach each other in value, a potential crossover may be forming, meaning that the momentum of the current trend is slowing and that the market is getting ready to correct, or even reverse. Likewise, as a trend strengthens, the moving averages move farther apart, indicating a continuation of the trend and an increase in momentum. When the two lines are remaining roughly parallel and moving in the same direction, this means that the trend is healthy and is an excellent indication that you should not micromanage the trade, but should let your profit run. From a directional standpoint, a crossover of the two averages can be used to confirm a short-term trend shift.

The MACD histogram is also another way to measure momentum, as it is the difference between the two averages. When the bars on the histogram are moving away from the zero level, it is seen as positive momentum; when they are moving toward the zero line, momentum is decreasing. Positive momentum indicates that the current trend is strengthening, and negative momentum indicates that the trend is weakening. It is important to also recognize that a slowing of momentum, more often than not, indicates a price pause, or correction, not a reversal. A shift in the MACD histogram, such as a decrease following a series of increases in a price uptrend or an increase following a series of decreases in a price downtrend, can be seen as the first indication of a potential shift in price direction. From a directional standpoint, we can say that a move below the centerline by the MACD—the black line in Exhibit 4-2—indicates a shift in a market's intermediate-term trend.

The MACD and MACD histogram give us indications or trade filters in several different ways, including a MACD centerline crossover (potential shift in the intermediate-term trend), a MACD moving average crossover (confirmation of a short-term trend shift), a MACD histogram shift (pause or shift in momentum), and both MACD and MACD histogram divergence (longer-term divergence

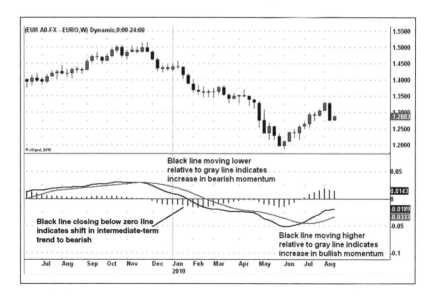

Exhibit 4-2
Source: www.esignal.com.

between price and momentum). In conducting our overview, we are going to focus primarily on a MACD moving average crossover; which side of the zero line the MACD is on, which helps us to determine a market's intermediate-term trend; and how the indicator measures divergence between price and momentum.

When the MACD crosses its trigger line, meaning that the 12-bar EMA crosses the 26-bar EMA, it is marked by a histogram zero-line cross, and it is generally going to confirm a short-term trend shift in price. We can call this occurrence a MACD cross. In simplistic terms, when the MACD is below its trigger line, it supports a short position, and when it's above its trigger line, it supports a long position. When the MACD crosses the zero line, it often marks an intermediate-term trend. We can see this dynamic play out in Exhibit 4-2.

We can classify a MACD bull cross above the zero line as a short-term trend shift in line with the intermediate-term trend, and a MACD bull cross below the zero line as a short-term trend shift counter to the intermediate-term trend. Likewise, a MACD bear cross below the zero line would be considered a trend move, and a MACD bear cross above the zero line would be considered a countertrend move. Also notice how when the two lines of the MACD are moving in the same direction, price tends to hold its trend as seen in Exhibit 4-3. This is telling us that momentum is steady and favoring a continuation of the trend. When the black line pulls away from the gray line this generally tells us price momentum is increasing.

The rate of change between the two lines (the MACD and the trigger line) gives us an indication of the strength of a move and is represented by the vertical bars, or histograms, that populate the center line of the indicator. If the distance between the two lines is increasing, the move underway is considered strong, and the histogram will show successively higher bars; if the distance between the two lines is decreasing, then the momentum of the move is waning, and the histogram will record shorter bars. This information is

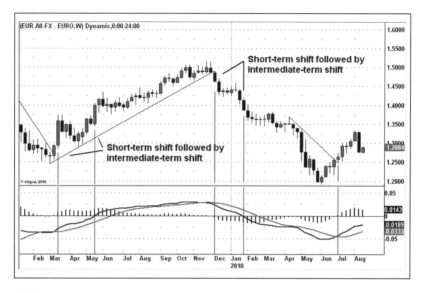

Exhibit 4-3
Source: www.esignal.com.

valuable in deciding to let a profit run if the MACD histogram is
increasing in the direction of our trade. Likewise, if you are in a
trade and the histogram is moving against your position, it would
be a warning that price momentum is starting to work against your
position.

Another way the MACD functions is to show divergence. Divergence occurs when price is going in one direction and the MACD, or
another momentum measuring indicator, is not confirming that direction. Price can be making lower lows, but if the rate of change is slowing over time, this will show up as higher lows, or even a flattening
MACD. This can telegraph a price pause or even a price reversal. This
is known as positive divergence between price and the MACD. Negative divergence occurs when price is still rising, but our MACD and
trigger line are moving sideways or falling. In strong market moves, it
is not uncommon to see double or even triple divergence before we
see a correction or reversal.

As a rule of thumb, divergence over a shorter time period is more powerful than divergence over a longer time period. Think of divergence as a development that tells us that a market needs to take a break. It is reasonable to consider that there will be times in a bear market when a market becomes oversold and momentum starts to wane, so that a correction is needed. Price is technically still moving lower, but momentum is slowing. Price may backtrack and test resistance before continuing on. While most market reversals exhibit divergence before they turn, they also exhibit this behavior just prior to normal consolidation periods.

In our analysis, we will also see divergence between the MACD histogram and price. Just as the divergence between price and the MACD line can be significant, the divergence between the histogram and price can also be significant.

Traders often ask, "Which divergence we should look for, that between the MACD cross (the black and grey lines) and price, or between the MACD histogram and price?" The answer is either one; however, short-term divergence will generally show up first on the histogram and can be more significant.

After gauging the current price trend on the chart, we look for the direction of the MACD to confirm that trend by monitoring the direction of the lines. We gauge the momentum of the trend through the MACD histogram. We are also aware of which side of the zero line the MACD is on because this helps us determine the market's intermediate-term trend. For trade signals, we want to have the MACD histogram moving in the same direction as the trade. Once we are in the trade, we monitor the MACD histogram, and if momentum increases in our favor, we stay in the trade to let the profit run. Should we get a MACD cross against our position on the same time frame we took the signal on, along with a trendline and directional shift, we almost assuredly would take that as a signal to exit the trade.

To summarize how we use the MACD, we use it to identify the trend, along with possible turning points or shifts in momentum, and to keep us in a trend trade longer, that is, to let a profit run. For countertrend trades, we look for divergence between the MACD and/or the MACD histogram and price. Knowing which side of the zero line the MACD is on helps us to quickly identify the intermediate-term trend, and prior to entering a trade, we always want to know the MACD's stance relative to its trigger line to determine whether momentum is favoring the signal or not. We can record any of this information in our trading plan checklist prior to trading. Over the course of this book, we refer many times to the importance of having price pattern, structure, and momentum in favor of your trade selections, and the MACD indicator is how we determine momentum.

Divergence between Price and Momentum

There are very definite indications when a trend is coming to an end, and while it is important that traders seek out primarily trend trades, it is also important that we learn to recognize those times when the trend could be stalling so that we can at least take defensive action. The MACD is going to be very helpful for identifying these times. Anytime we see a MACD cross with steep angulation on the higher-time-frame chart, and divergence between price and momentum on a lower-time-frame chart, we need to be aware of the increasing likelihood of a price reversal. More often than not, though, initial divergence on the lower time frames, which is defined by price extending a move, but on less and less momentum (think of a ball rolling uphill) means a correction or a price pause.

There are two types of divergence between price and momentum, and this categorization depends on whether the market we are analyzing is in an uptrend or a downtrend. In an uptrend, when we see price making a higher high and the momentum indicator making a lower high, this is called *negative divergence*. In a downtrend, when we see price making a lower low while the momentum indicator is making a higher low, this is called *positive divergence*. Divergence definitely needs to be identified, recorded, and included in our overview.

Divergence on the Higher Time Frames

In Exhibit 4-4, we see the MACD cross lower on the weekly chart in the lower panel after a buildup of negative divergence on the daily chart on top—notice that as price makes a higher high, the MACD is making a lower high. Given that this occurred on higher-time-frame charts, we saw an actual reversal follow. The higher the time frame it occurs on, the more seriously we need to take this form of divergence. We also need to remember that initial divergence is more often a sign that the market needs a breather before a resumption of a move,

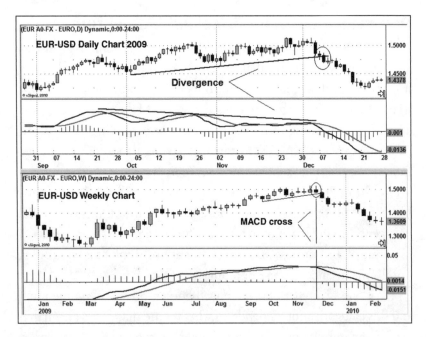

Exhibit 4-4
Source: www.esignal.com.

whereas double or even triple divergence is an indication that we may want to pass on taking a new trade in the same direction as the current trend, or as a sign to tighten stops or even exit the trade on a change of direction on a lower time frame. Double, or triple divergence occurs when a price trend continues to extend itself making multiple new highs, or lows, while the momentum indicator, MACD, is recording lower highs, or in the case of a downtrend, higher lows. While divergence is legitimate reference information, it is not actionable intelligence. We still need to wait for a proper setup and signal, which we will cover in detail in Chapters 7 and 8.

Divergence on the Lower Time Frames

Exhibit 4-5 is a snapshot of the e-mini S&P 500 futures contract in September of 2010, where we see an uptrend on the top panel of the 240-minute chart and a buildup of negative divergence on the MACD in the lower panel. In this situation, both the weekly and daily charts

Exhibit 4-5
Source: www.esignal.com.

were pointed higher, and the divergence on the intraday charts signaled a pause, or a sideways move during the last week of the month, before price pressed higher. In a case like this, where the trends on the daily and weekly charts are higher and showing no divergence, you can actually look at negative divergence on the lower time frames as confirmation of the overall uptrend. What this is telling us is that after the trend establishes itself, it needs a breather, and the countertrend move produced by any reaction lower is likely to be fading as the higher-time-frame trends reassert themselves. It's an important distinction to make that we are more likely to see divergence toward the end of both short-term and long-term trends, making this an important consideration in your trading.

If you are seeing divergence, it's telling you that the move is not beginning but maturing, and maturing trends generally give us bigger moves than budding trends. Divergence is a way to help us gauge the age of a trend, and when we see it on the intraday time frames, it can mean that the overall trend still has a ways to go, while when we see it on the weekly chart, it can tell us that the move is coming to an end.

Pretrade Checklist Revisited

Once we've recorded the short-term trends on the different time frames and recorded any divergence or price patterns that we might see on the various charts, we are in a position to choose which markets are best for us to trade. We need to focus on markets where the trends are coordinated on the higher time frames and are giving us coordinating strength or weakness readings based on their daily or weekly net change readings, and seek out trades in that same direction. This is called directional trading. Realistically, though, we don't always have that option.

If the markets we trade are not coordinated on the higher time frames or are in broad sideways patterns, we have three choices: don't trade, swing trade, or trade lower time frames. While trading higher time frames gives the trader the most favorable risk/reward scenario, day trading can lead to the highest winning percentage, because trading the lowest time frames, 15- and 3-minute charts, can still mean having higher-time-frame confirmation on the 60- or 240-minute charts for those times when the weekly and daily charts or the monthly and weekly charts are counter to each other. Swing trading definitely has its advantages in a countertrending market because rather than take only signals with higher-time-frame confirmation, we can take all the signals as they occur. The monthly and weekly trends that are in place in a market are extremely influential and dictate direction on the daily and hourly time frames. Time frames as low as a 5-minute or 3-minute chart, however, with directional confirmation from a 15-minute chart, are low enough in time to not be as influenced by the dominant time frames. While trend shifts on the daily or hourly time frames can prove treacherous for position or swing traders, trading the 3- and 15-minute time frames can put you in a position to take advantage of these same moves. A big advantage of the method we are teaching you now is that the rules are the same, whether you are trading the 3- and 15-minute charts or trading the daily and weekly charts.

We've given you a lot of information and a tactic to keep it all organized, in the form of your pretrade checklist. You will see that the checklist is a great exercise to see how serious you are about your trading, because you should expect to fill it out every day before you even consider placing a trade.

Multiple Time Frames and Higher Time Frames Revisited

Before we get lured into overanalyzing markets, or "analysis paralysis," it's important to remember that there are always three trends at play in the market: the short-term, the intermediate-term, and the long-term.

So in addition to the time-frame chart you are trading, there are always two additional time frames you can use to determine if a signal has higher-time-frame confirmation. The next higher time frame to the one we are considering trading represents the intermediate-term trend, and two time frames higher represents the long-term trend. So if we are going to take a trade on the daily chart, we could opt for confirmation on the weekly chart, where the current trend would be the rough equivalent of the intermediate-term trend on the daily chart; or we could use the monthly chart for confirmation, where the current trend would represent the approximate long-term trend on the daily chart. A good rule of thumb is, if you are at a significant confluence of higher-time-frame structure—(support or resistance), or if there is significant fundamental news breaking, then use the intermediate-term time frame to confirm the trade on the time frame you are taking the trigger on, or don't even wait for confirmation and just take the signal as it occurs on your short-term chart.

If there is no impending news and price is not at significant support or resistance, then wait for confirmation from the long-term trend. For example, if you are trading a 15-minute chart, you have the choice of using the current price action on the 60-minute chart, that is, the intermediate-term trend, to filter your trade, or you can use the current price action on the 240-minute chart, that is, the long-term trend, to filter your trade. When you use the current candle on the intermediate-term time-frame chart, you need to know that you are making a decision based on an unclosed candle. You can also base your decision on the previous closed candle on the higher time frame. Here the same rule of thumb would apply. If you are at significant support or resistance, and/or if there is influential economic news breaking, then use your lowest-time-frame chart for the setup and signal, or at least the next higher-time-frame chart, meaning the intermediate-term time frame, even though the candle on the intermediate-term chart may not be closed.

If price action is slower, however, and price is in between structure (price is between the pivots and/or trendlines, or in "no man's land," as we call it), then use the closed candle on the higher-time-frame chart to make your decision. The indicators that we use at www.trading-u.com are designed to give us a directional reading on any individual time frame or combination that we deem appropriate from the short-term, intermediate-term, or long-term trends, and from current price action on the higher-time-frame candle or confirmation from the previous closed candle on the higher time frames.

Higher time frames are for determining which markets to trade and which direction to trade them from, for confirming direction before entering a trade, and for helping to manage a trade (that is, let a profit run) or exiting a trade. Lower time frames are for protecting equity once you are in the trade and for countertrend trading. The primary information that you need from a higher-time-frame chart is confirmation of a trade signal on a lower time frame. Ideally, you would have both a directional-line shift and a trendline break on the higher time frame; the rule of thumb, however, for higher-time-frame confirmation would be a trendline break and/or a directional-line shift.

Using lower time frames to manage a trade and protect equity is also fairly straightforward. When price comes upon significant support or resistance, and shows indecisive behavior, we can use a trade signal on that lower time frame to exit our position or a portion of our position. Once we take one-half to two-thirds of our position off, we manage the balance of the position on the higher-time-frame chart. We cover this concept in more detail in Chapter 9. The key thing to remember when using multiple time frames is not to over-analyze the situation. If you are trading off 15-minute and 3-minute charts, do not be concerned with divergence on a 60-minute chart; trade only what is happening on the right side of the two time frames you are using.

Recap

In these past two chapters, we've given you a lot of information on the different steps that go into a market overview. Now we need to boil it down so that you can put it to use quickly and easily. The key to trading, as with so many things in life, is working smarter, not necessarily harder. Taking what you've learned in this chapter and using it to organize your decision-making process may be easier if we break the key components down to bullet points:

- Take a daily chart with from eight months to a year of data on it and mark the monthly highs and lows, and/or draw straight channel trendlines if they fit the price pattern. Then record the direction of the pattern in your Pretrade Checklist. Remember that the current pattern may be different from the overall pattern.
- Determine a market's current direction by marking the trendline and directional line on a single time frame—for example, the daily chart—and define this time frame as the short-term trend.
- Repeat this process for the market's intermediate- and long-term charts—for example, if we are considering the daily chart to be short-term, then we consider the current trend on the weekly chart to be the intermediate-term trend of the daily chart, and the current trend on the monthly chart to be the long-term trend on the daily chart.
- Record the nearest structure (trendlines, pivot points, directional lines, and retracements) on all the different time-frame charts.
- Identify momentum and/or divergence on the different time frames.
- Collate this information in a format that is simple to access and view—a spreadsheet or chart.

By following these steps regularly, you are going to put yourself in a much more organized state, which will go a long way toward helping you to maintain that focused, yet relaxed state while you are awaiting trade setups and triggers.

For further examples of trade setups on color charts, go to www.trading-u.com/tradeselection.asp.

Chapter 5

FUNDAMENTALS OF RISK AND PRICE MOVEMENT

The most important aspect of market fundamentals is people—more specifically, demographics. On a yearly timeline, it's much more important to know how many people are entering the workforce compared to the number leaving the workforce and how many people on average are getting married and having children than it is to know a retail sales number or a monthly consumer price index. A country's social behavior on a year-over-year basis will always trump its month-to-month economic behavior in the eyes of professional investors. Demographics are so important because in general they are predictable year to year. Let's look at the projected population pyramid for Australia for 2012 in Exhibit 5-1, as supplied by the U.S. Census Bureau. This simple chart shows the country's population distribution by age group.

The surge in the number of people between the ages of 20 and 40 ensures that Australia will have a much larger consumer and investor class than it will have retirees for many years to come. Think of the economic activity of the 20-year-olds going forward as they enter the workforce, then start to pair off and marry, then start to save and invest, and to have children (who will also grow up to become consumers). That's impressive. With so many more younger people than aging folks, Australia is assured of healthy demographics for many years to come. The implications for the real estate and stock markets

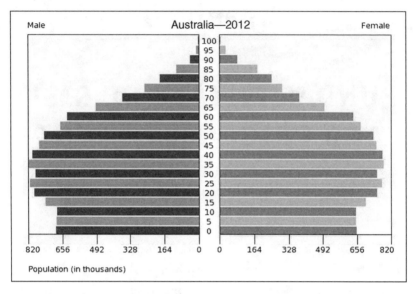

Exhibit 5-1
Source: U.S. Bureau of the Census, www.census.gov.

in that country are significant also. As people age, they start to downsize their property and their homes, and they start to move out of riskier investments such as stocks and into fixed-income securities. With so many younger people coming up through the age ranks, there will be plenty of buyers for those assets as the seniors start to scale back.

The Japanese pyramid in Exhibit 5-2 shows a completely different demographic. Here we see a two-tier investor class, with the largest portion of the population being between 60 and 65, and with the age group just coming into the workforce, 20- to 25-year-olds, being disproportionately small.

This population mix makes for a not-so-certain demographic. As seniors retire and try to downsize their homes and move their investments from riskier equity markets to fixed income, there won't be enough younger people to step up and buy. Japan's current 35- to 45-year-old investor class is still powerful, but without a sizable population of young

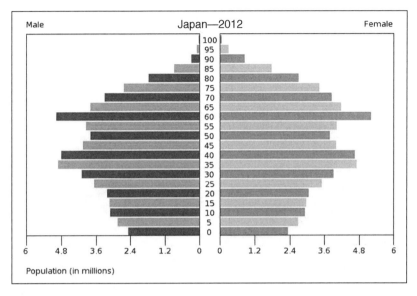

Exhibit 5-2
Source: U.S. Bureau of the Census, www.census.gov.

consumers coming into the workforce, businesses that rely on this market segment must be very competitive, leaving smaller and smaller profit margins. We can see plainly that over the next 20 years, Japan must adjust to a shrinking population—not a good thing from a long-term investor's standpoint.

For all the talk on blogs and newsletters about the eventual sinking of the U.S. economy because of deep-seated economic problems, the U.S. population pyramid (Exhibit 5-3) doesn't look too bad, particularly when compared to those of Japan, Canada, and many European countries.

While there is a slight drop-off below the 50- to 55-year-old bracket, the population is fairly evenly distributed, and actually well represented at that important 20- to 25-year-old range. Compare this to Switzerland's population pyramid (Exhibit 5-4), where we see a very small up-and-coming consumer class.

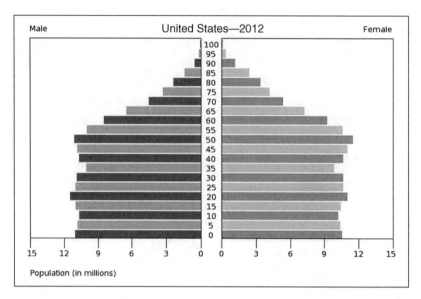

Exhibit 5-3

Source: U.S. Bureau of the Census, www.census.gov.

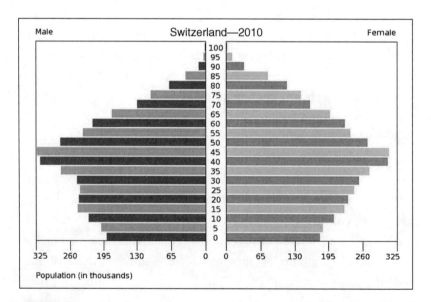

Exhibit 5-4

Source: U.S. Bureau of the Census, www.census.gov.

There's no doubt that demographics are a very important consideration for an investor with a long-range outlook, and help to explain why we see such long, steady price trends for stocks, bonds, and currencies. They will not, however, help in recognizing when market corrections, or even reversals, are occurring. For this we need to understand month in, month out economic developments, or, more to the point, understand the intermediate- and shorter-term economic developments that create the risk component that individual markets must factor in.

Fundamental News = Risk

The hardest part of teaching you how to factor fundamental developments into your trading is getting you to first understand and then "feel" the risk element brought on by economic releases and reports. As we move forward with this lesson, you will start to see that fundamental economic events equate to risk or nonrisk for an individual market, and we don't know the degree to which that risk will affect a market until after the event or news is disseminated among the players that trade that market. Before we can address economic risk, however, we need to put it in the perspective of price.

How can we measure the risk of a negative report or the nonrisk of a positive report unless we can measure how much the market moved as a percentage of price? To understand the effect of the risk, we also need to gauge the price movement it caused relative to the existing price pattern and longer-term direction. Exhibit 5-5 provides an example of this following the lower-than-expected November 2010 employment release on December 3, 2010. The S&P 500 stock-index futures contract was in an uptrend prior to the release. The nonfarm payroll number came out 100,000 employees less than expected, increasing the risk of holding long positions in a U.S. stock index, and price fell sharply.

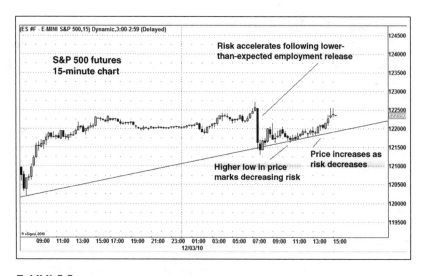

Exhibit 5-5
Source: www.esignal.com.

Price moved lower initially because of the increase in risk, but it bottomed just one candle later and started to slowly recover. As this market recovered, we can say that the risk of being long was decreasing. Once the risk decreases to the point where the majority of traders feel that the potential from being long outweighs the risk, price accelerates higher. What is very important to see in this example is that the price pattern—trend—that was in place before the employment release was higher. Although the news release increased the risk of being long this market, the risk was counter to the existing price pattern. Because the existing price pattern was higher, the downdraft created by the report—the risk—was more likely to be a correction than a reversal.

In Exhibit 5-6, we have an example of the results of an economic release that was in line with the existing price pattern. On December 2 at 10:00 a.m. EDT, the U.S. National Association of Realtors released a month-over-month pending home sales report showing a whopping 10.4 percent increase. The S&P 500 stock index futures were already in an uptrend, which then accelerated, as the economic release caused

Exhibit 5-6
Source: www.esignal.com.

a sharp decrease in the risk of being long a U.S. stock index. The existing uptrend, coupled with the decrease in risk, powered the market to still higher highs throughout the remainder of the session.

Fundamental Events Create Risk

We need to understand how risk, or lack of risk, is created by economic releases and new events, how this is measured in terms of price action, and, most important, how we as traders need to react to fundamental developments. There are two assertions that we make that help us to coordinate fundamental news and economic releases and developments into our trading:

1. It is fundamental economic developments that propel the business cycle, and the business cycle provides the overriding framework for market price action. Therefore, a market's price pattern, or wave cycle, is a reflection of the business cycle.

2. Because investment bankers, money managers, and professional speculators have more of an immediate interest in price outcome than the government statisticians who compile the fundamental economic information, and because the majority of professional traders key off of how price action reacts to economic data, rather than the data themselves, price will often lead the business cycle.

The first assertion is self-explanatory. The second assertion means that because of the importance of economic data to investors and traders, there will always be economic consulting firms that collect and collate economic data using the same techniques as the U.S. Census Bureau, the U.S. Commerce Department, and other government agencies use, if not better techniques. This is how many banks and brokers are able to put out forecasts that regularly come within less than 0.5 percent of the actual releases. Former U.S. Federal Reserve Chairman Alan Greenspan ran such a firm from the 1960s through the 1980s, where he was widely regarded as one of Wall Street's most accurate economic forecasters.

It is also worth noting in the second assertion that "the majority of professional traders key off of how price action reacts to economic data, rather than the data themselves." Once you start to trade, you will understand why that is. It is the goal of every professional trader to balance increasing the rate of return on his trading account with the protection of his principal. In doing so, a trader will react to his falling account balance more quickly than he will ponder why a market is moving in the opposite direction from what the economic release just seemingly indicated. There is an old market adage that professional traders live by: "Cut your losses and let your profits run." This means that traders are much quicker to react when a market is moving against their position than they are when price is moving in their favor.

Although we spend much more time prepping you with technical information in this book, so that you know those specific points in time and price when you can enter trades with confidence, we know from our own trading experience that we rely on fundamental information more than we sometimes realize. There are several things that we check off in considering a day trade or a swing trade, and at the top of that list is "check economic calendar." First, we must know when the significant economic events (aka risk) are scheduled, and second, we must take an unbiased look at how price reacts to those events. If a German economic report comes out much worse than expected, and the EUR-USD shows little reaction to it, and actually holds its current bullish price pattern and starts to uptick, we would take this as a sign of strength and favor buy signals. Our reason is clear-cut: the economic release came out worse than expected and was bearish for EUR-USD; however, price rejected the increased risk and did not show an overly bearish reaction, but in fact held its current bullish price pattern. This tells us nearly instantly that the majority of active traders in this market who heed fundamental news are probably already short or at least not interested in selling the EUR-USD despite negative news. If they are already short and they got what they had hoped for, bad news, but price still starts to move against them, then they are more likely to cover their shorts or buy to avoid losses, that is, protect their principal. This is exactly what happened in Exhibit 5.7, which is a snapshot of the EUR-USD on September 8, 2010.

The German industrial production number came in a full percentage point lower than expected, yet price held the overall bullish price pattern in place before the release—risk—and then gave a buy signal. We can see from the bull trendline below price and how the stochastic behaved that both structure and momentum supported the buy signal and trumped the potential increase in risk. Professional traders who are already positioned in the market are not as interested in the actual fundamental news as they are in how price reacts to that news.

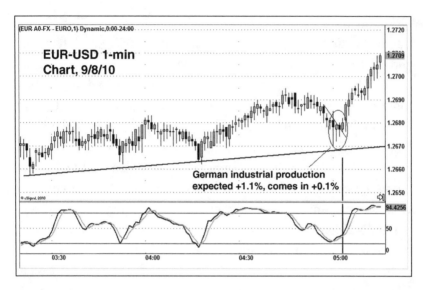

Exhibit 5-7
Source: www.esignal.com.

Let Price Interpret Risk

In *Mastering the Currency Market* (McGraw-Hill, 2009), we did a thorough job of defining fundamental analysis and demonstrating how it affects markets, but not necessarily how it affects traders. This is an important distinction to make, and one that we need to make clear. Raw economic data influence both the current and future decision-making processes of companies that are end users of the commodities and financial products that we trade. The decisions made by the officers of these companies affect market prices over time. Market pricing is what most professional discretionary traders react to. Therefore, most directional traders are actually a step removed from what are commonly referred to as "the fundamentals."

Likewise, if a trading decision is made following an economic release that indicates a shift in or a continuation of specific market conditions, it would be unreasonable to think that, from a trader's perspective, one would stay in that trade until similar economic data indicated that a change had in fact taken place, given the open trade equity of a live trade and the difficulty of protecting one's principal for an unspecified period of time. Such a strategy could leave the speculator open to unlimited losses in a profession in which defined risk is essential. One of the surest ways to lose money as a speculator, in our experience, is to stay in a losing trade and wait for fundamental conditions to confirm that the position was ill timed, that is, the trader's decision to initiate the trade was wrong. This is why we allow price to interpret fundamental data for us first, and then react to risk and price.

As traders, we are not analysts or economists; our only job is to position ourselves in the same direction that the market is currently moving. If price movement is in line with current economic data—that is, if we are long a basket of U.S. blue chip stocks, the monthly employment number comes in higher than expected, and price confirms the decrease in risk by moving higher—we maintain our position. If price is moving against our position despite what we would interpret as supportive fundamental news, we acknowledge that risk is working against our position and take down the sails (exit the position).

Don't Fight the Fed

"The more things change, the more they stay the same" is an appropriate saying with regard to financial market fundamentals. The same sayings we heard on the floor of the Chicago Board of Trade or in a brokerage firm's lounge in the 1980s are being heard today by a younger generation of traders, and they hold just as true. Whether the chairman is Paul Volcker, Alan Greenspan, or Ben Bernanke, "Don't fight the Fed" is still good advice to heed. From a trader's perspective, the fundamental events that shape the business and political cycles should be observed, but not weighed for too long. Despite our own weakness for occasionally getting lured into expressing a market opinion on the various media outlets we participate in, it is definitely not for a trader to reason why. This is because when it comes to gauging price action based on what we read from economic releases, such as the Federal Open Market Committee's statements or the monthly non-farm payroll numbers, we just can't afford to be wrong. And the number one rule when it comes to gauging the effects of a fundamental event on a market is: don't argue with price if it's gone beyond your predetermined risk point. If you are on the losing end of a trade and you disagree with what price is doing, you had better recognize that it's probably you who is wrong, not the market.

The number one fundamental event in the financial marketplace as of this writing is how central bankers and treasurers are taking an active role in managing interest rates and the money supply in an effort to balance slowing economies and rising government debt levels. Following the G-20 meeting in the summer of 2010, the U.S. economic team appeared to be at odds with the other members of the G-20, with the United States opting for continued low interest rates with plans for quick stimulation if needed and putting off government deficit reduction plans until economic growth gains traction. The U.S. plan is called "quantitative easing" by most media outlets. The Europeans (the Germans in particular), along with the British and Canadians, favored deficit reduction, which probably means higher interest rates and less of a "hands-on" nurturing of their economies. The Japanese have already made up their minds on which road to take by carrying the highest public debt levels and lowest interest-rate levels of any advanced economy.

Textbook economics tells us that money will flow to the currency with the highest interest rate. Given that the Japanese have the lowest interest rates of any industrialized nation and the Europeans are talking about stricter money controls, which currency do you think would be stronger? Rather than attempt to answer that question and get into

Exhibit 5-8
Source: www.esignal.com.

analyzing how governments stand on these important issues coming out of the summer of 2010, let's look at a weekly chart of EUR-JPY as of August 2010 in Exhibit 5-8.

Keep in mind that at this time, the Europeans are opting for less debt and possibly tighter monetary conditions, while the Japanese have lived with extremely low interest rates and ballooning government debt for many years. Yet, as we can see on the chart, the European currency continues to weaken against the Japanese currency. Why? From a professional trader's perspective, the answer is, "Who cares?" Trading is not about "why"; it's about having a plan and executing that plan. The point of the response "Who cares?" is that knowing why investors are favoring long yen positions and short euro positions, or, more specifically, why Japanese investors are exiting their euro holdings, is not necessary in order to make money as a trader. What is necessary from our perspective is to know that the current trend on the chart is lower, and to know what point in price and time would need to be eclipsed to change the direction of that trend.

Would we want to know if the Japanese plan on intervening in their currency by selling it and when because an expensive currency creates a serious drag on exports? Sure. But it is extremely unlikely that we would find out this information far enough ahead of the rest of the market for it to be useful. Our good friend Bill Williams, the author of *Trading Chaos* (Wiley, 1995), often referred to a trader trying to connect the dots of fundamental developments and then apply this to her trading as "mental masturbation." We agree with that assessment. You need to know when price is valuing or discounting the risk of economic developments in the context of the current price pattern and direction. The way to keep track of this is to watch how a market reacts to the different economic reports, and note when price is moving in line with risk and when it is not. Exhibit 5-9 provides a good example of this.

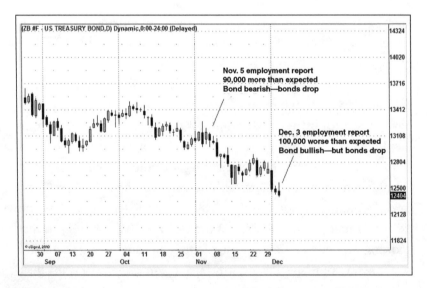

Exhibit 5-9
Source: www.esignal.com.

On November 5, the U.S. nonfarm payroll came out 90,000 higher than expected, and price gave a predictable reaction by moving lower—when employment increases, this is consistent with higher interest rates; therefore, bonds move lower. One month later, the same employment figure came out down 100,000, a particularly bullish number. Price initially rallied, which is consistent with expectations (lower employment rates equate to lower interest rates), but then topped out and turned lower through the rest of the day to close down on the day. It's very important for traders to recognize when markets are shrugging off the way they are "expected" to react so that they can position themselves to take advantage of actual price movement, rather than being stuck in a losing position because "price isn't reacting the way it should." We think it's significant that price was exhibiting a clear bearish pattern of lower highs and lower lows before that second release, so despite the "bullish" economic number, traders were already predisposed to play the short side.

As we touched on in Chapter 1, the last thing you want to do when you observe significant economic developments is fall into the trap of weighing their effects too heavily and then trying to gauge the reasoning or timing behind them. As you might imagine, people who feel a need to know the "why" of events such as the supply and demand of grain products, or the reasons and mechanics behind international currency flows, generally don't make decisions quickly enough, with enough conviction, to make good traders; similarly, traders don't always make good businesspeople because they are not in the habit of researching things more thoroughly, and they don't have the same process in place for decisions outside the trading realm.

Don't take us the wrong way; it's great to know what's influencing the markets and why, particularly if it dovetails with your own trading success, but this isn't something that you should expect to happen right out of the gate in your trading journey. It's better not to be concerned if you don't understand the "why" of price movement or you can't find a story in the news relating what price did to a news event or release. There are more important things you need to work on than knowing the underlying or overriding economic events behind market movement. You will find that trade management in a live market, even if only in a demo account, will be infinitely more useful to you than pondering the European Central Bank's next move. It is far more important to know when fundamental news is going to hit the market than it is to guess how that news will affect the market. There is a built-in advantage to knowing when the risk will occur, and a real disadvantage to anticipating how the market will interpret the risk. Professional traders are much more apt to trim their positions or even flatten out ahead of such influential releases as central bankers' interest-rate announcements and other economic releases than they are to actually trade based on the releases.

Most institutional traders, also known as "house traders," who trade every day aren't directional traders at all but market makers. They make profits not by trying to buy low and sell high, but by taking the other side of as many trades as they can. Their goal is to take the money that directional traders are attempting to make. On days when volume in the markets is high, the house traders do well because they can take the other side of more trades. These days often coincide with major government releases such as durable goods orders, retail sales, or GDP numbers. Professional traders refer to price action following news releases as "amateur hour" because this is when amateur traders get lured into the markets because they think this is what they should be doing.

Traders who have been around the block a few times understand that economic numbers trend also. And there is no doubt that it is the trends in the actual raw fundamental data that create the business cycle, but just as with individual candles or bars on a chart, we know that one report does not make a trend. There are times when an individual report is worth noting, but for the most part it is the direction of the trend of the economic data that is important to us. The attention that is paid to individual economic releases by the news services, blog community, and retail trading population is definitely overstated.

As we've said, it's more important to know when incoming information (that is, risk) is going to hit the market than it is to guess what the information will be and how the market will react to it. It's also important to know which information is influential so that you can make sure that you don't get caught in a situation where you have to exit a trade, not because your plan tells you to, but because significant news is impending. It's also a good idea to review any economic numbers that may have come out earlier in the session, before you trade, to see how price reacted to them. This is more for reference than actionable information, but you will want to know those times where price responded differently from what a release may have dictated. Before we get ahead of ourselves, though, let's go over the specific economic releases that market participants respect the most, and cover those financial markets that we know to be leading indicator markets.

Key Economic Reports

Major economic news releases are available at any number of online sites. We use www.ForexFactory.com. On the front page of its Web site, there is a tab for Calendar. If you click on that tab, it will show an extended list of economic releases for the week and their expected impact. Releases coded red have the highest expected level of impact. Another great resource is www.munibondadvisor.com/EconomicIndicators.htm. This site has links directly to the source for every news release.

In Exhibit 5-10, we compiled a summary spreadsheet of the most influential news releases for the United States, including the typical release dates and the net effect that the release may have on the U.S. dollar and/or the stock market. Please note that these are generalizations

Key Economic Reports

Report	Change	Dollar Friendly	Dollar Unfriendly	Release Date
Nonfarm payroll	Payroll increases	X		The first Friday of every month at 8:30 a.m. EST
	Payroll decreases		X	
FOMC	Interest rates increase	X		Release time varies —meets 8 times per year
	Interest rates decrease		X	
Retail sales	Sales increase	X		Midmonth, usually around the 13th at 8:30 a.m. EST
	Sales decrease		X	
Durable goods	Factory orders increase	X		Twice per month at 8:30 a.m. EST
	Factory orders decrease		X	
Gross domestic product	Increase in GDP	X		Quarterly on the 25th of the month at 8:30 a.m. EST
	Decrease in GDP		X	
Producer Price Index	Prices increase	X		The third week of each month at 10:00 a.m. EST
	Prices decrease		X	
Consumer Price Index	Prices increase	X		Mid-month at 8:30 a.m. EST
	Prices decrease		X	
Consumer confidence	Spending increases	X		The last Tuesday of every month at 10:00 a.m. EST
	Spending decreases		X	

Leading Indicators

Report	Change	Dollar Friendly	Dollar Unfriendly
The S&P 500	Index value increases	X	
	Index value decreases		X
U.S. T-bonds and notes	Value increases		X
	Value decreases	X	

Exhibit 5-10

and are only one factor affecting market price. We do not recommend that anyone to trade ahead of a major news release, as the results can be extreme and unpredictable. Following our summary spreadsheet, we have included a discussion of each factor along with charts and examples for the more influential reports.

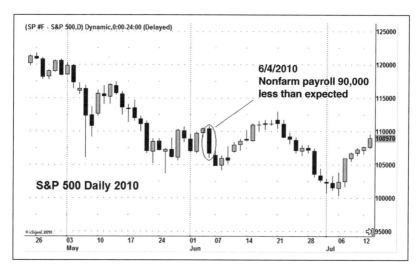

Exhibit 5-11
Source: www.esignal.com.

Nonfarm payroll. This reports the number of jobs added to or
subtracted from the U.S. economy in the nonagricultural
sectors over the previous month. It is released on the first
Friday of the month. It can have an outsized effect on markets
because it is considered to be a very influential indicator of
economic health (see Exhibit 5-11). This number is reported
by the U.S. Department of Labor, Bureau of Labor Statistics,
www.bls.gov.

The Federal Open Market Committee. The Federal Open Market
Committee, or FOMC, holds considerable sway over all financial markets, as it is this governing body of the Federal Reserve
Board that sets interest-rate policy. The committee reports on
interest-rate decisions by the Federal Reserve Bank (the Fed)
and gives traders valuable insight into the Fed's decision-making
process through these reports. It meets eight times per year, and
there is an announcement following the close of each meeting.
A change in the federal funds rate (the rate at which banks lend

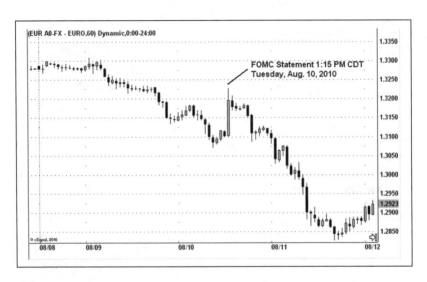

(EUR A0-FX - EURO,60) Dynamic,0:00-24:00

FOMC Statement 1:15 PM CDT
Tuesday, Aug. 10, 2010

Exhibit 5-12
Source: www.esignal.com.

money to each other) as mandated by the Fed affects interest rates across the board and can have a major impact on business decisions across a wide range of businesses and industries. The results of the FOMC meetings can be found on the Federal Reserve Web site at www.federalreserve.gov. Always remember that in general, a decision to raise interest rates would be bullish for the U.S. dollar, and a decision to lower rates would be bearish for the U.S. dollar. An example of the market reaction to an FOMC statement is shown in Exhibit 5-12.

Durable goods. This monthly report tells us the value of orders received by U.S. domestic manufacturers for big-ticket items with a life expectancy of more than three years, such as motor vehicles, appliances, and even computers. The release comes out at the end of every month and is compiled from a variety of sources. The figures on durable goods are released by the U.S. Census Bureau and can be found on its Web site at http://www.census.gov/indicator/www/m3/. Exhibit 5-13 shows a chart of the S&P 500 stock

(ES #F - E-MINI S&P 500,15) Dynamic,3:00-2:59 (Delayed)

Stock market shrugs off -2.7% core durable goods orders

Exhibit 5-13
Source: www.esignal.com.

index for the same period in which a surprisingly weak durable goods figure was released. The market, which was moving higher at the time, quickly shrugged off the negative economic release (which came in at minus 2.7 percent when a positive 0.7 percent was expected), giving traders the green light to continue to work the long side. Textbook economics would tell us that a weaker-than-expected release would be bearish for stocks, yet in this case, traders determined very quickly that the risk introduced by that negative number was minimal and took the market's reaction as a sign to buy.

Retail sales. This monthly report gives us a reading on retail activity over the previous month, which gives us insight into consumer spending habits. The figures on retail sales are released by the U.S. Census Bureau and can be found on its Web site at www.census.gov.

Gross domestic product. Gross domestic product, or GDP, is a measure of national income and output for the economy. It is generally measured over the previous quarter and then annualized, so it tends to be a lagging indicator. The textbook definition of a recession is two straight quarters of negative GDP growth. We did not provide a chart example for U.S. GDP because the market rarely shows a strong reaction to a U.S. GDP release, having taken its measurements and made its reactions based on the more timely economic indicators.

The Producer Price Index. The Producer Price Index, or PPI, measures changes in prices received by producers for their output. It is a key indicator for determining inflation on the production level. This number is reported by the U.S. Department of Labor, Bureau of Labor Statistics, at www.bls.gov. Generally, a higher-than-expected U.S. PPI release lends itself to U.S. dollar strength, as the expectation is that interest rates will be raised to combat inflation.

The Consumer Price Index. The Consumer Price Index, or CPI, measures the average price of consumer goods and services bought by households. It is a key indicator for determining inflation on the retail level, as cost of living elements are factored into the prices. As with many other reports, there are multiple segments given, but it is best to focus on the core rate and avoid being distracted by other segments. This number is reported by the U.S. Department of Labor, Bureau of Labor Statistics, at www.bls.gov.

Consumer Confidence. This index measures the level of economic optimism of consumers based on their saving and spending activities and is generally released on the last Tuesday of the month by the Conference Board; see www.conference-board.org. As important as these reports and releases are, they are still only lagging indicators, as they generally give us the previous month's or quarter's activity. Generally a higher-than-expected consumer confidence reading would be read as being positive for U.S. stocks and the U.S. dollar.

What is important to understand about these economic releases is that if you are a lower-time-frame trader—a day trader—you do not want to enter positions just ahead of them because of the risk associated with their release. Because most professional traders, particularly arbitrage traders and market makers, do not trade ahead of influential economic events and releases, it is rare that a market would exhibit a large price move just ahead of such a release. If you do see an outsized price movement in your favor ahead of a news release, even if you are a longer-term position trader, you should consider taking off at least a portion of your position to take advantage of the move, as it is unlikely that price will continue in that direction because the move was made on light volume. In fact, more times than not, price will retrace back to where it was before the low-volume, high-volatility movement kicked off, erasing itself ahead of the release. This also means that many times, before an event such as a U.S. unemployment release or an economic summit, price will go into a holding pattern—a countertrend consolidation pattern—as traders flatten out positions ahead of the scheduled news.

Economic numbers, like market behavior itself, tend to trend. And there are also those times when trading volume is low and economic numbers can have an outsized effect on price. If you are an active trader, and you operate on the lower-time-frame charts (that is, day trade), you have probably experienced this. Often you will notice this happening during the London session first, where an economic release will come in a bit better or worse than expected and the currency markets will produce higher volatility, or price moves that are larger than normal, increasing risk. Most of the time this is due to low volume, meaning lower trader participation rates. Once traders see this happening early in the session, they are on guard for it as the trading day rolls into the U.S. session.

The same thing will happen when U.S. economic data come in a bit more or a bit less than expected; again, the markets will produce outsized moves. It is important that you recognize this because it is going to determine whether you carry positions through lesser anticipated economic releases, or how close to the release you will wait before exiting a trade. There are also times when trends are entrenched, trader participation rates are high, and the market shows very little reaction even to economic news that is beyond the guesstimates. To the untrained market student, this price action can appear random, even confusing. To traders who understand how markets ebb and flow and how events trend just as price does, this price action comes as no surprise.

And then there are those times when price gets it wrong and the fundamentals get it right. This can occur when the higher time frames, such as the 4-hour and daily charts, are pointing higher, an economic report is due out, and the guesstimate is in line with the previous report. The market may give a sell signal ahead of the report on an intraday chart, while the 4-hour and daily charts remain stubbornly higher, keeping higher-time-frame traders at bay. Then the report comes out a bit worse than the estimates, and the market shifts south all at once, leaving the longer-term players, who needed that higher-time-frame confirmation, on the sidelines.

While these different scenarios can sometimes appear to be random and confusing to an analyst who is trying to "attach" an economic event to a larger-than-average price move as a way of explaining to a client or a reporter why a market did what it did, more often, from the observation post of an experienced discretionary trader, they are easily explainable. For example, it could simply be a matter of knowing that the market (price) came into the session exhibiting a bearish directional pattern, and when a retracement rally of the current downtrend proved shallow, an economic release came in as expected (meaning that there was no surprise and decreasing risk for shorts), and price closed below structure—POW: price dropped sharply as traders raced one another to the "sell button" because they collectively knew that with the "news" out of the way, only two hours until lunch in New York, and price settling below structure (perhaps a pivot point), they had a sell signal with favorable timing and (because of the shallow retracement) an attractive risk/reward scenario. Did the news play a part in our decision-making process? Yes. Once it was "out of the way" and the risk was removed, we were clear to resume trading operations based on price only, not on questionable incoming information (risk). On the other hand, if the economic release was a surprise one way or the other, price would have reacted differently and we might or might not have gotten a favorable setup and signal. So while the news is a consideration, it's often more a speed bump than a directional determinant.

As discretionary traders, we are not reacting to the "news," we are reacting to how price is influenced by the news. We understand that there are computer models dictating what many trading funds will do based on the results of specific economic releases. And there are no doubt even other individual traders who are waiting to initiate or exit trades based specifically on the outcome of the releases. For us, however, the specific news is not nearly as important as how the next 3-minute candle or the next 15-minute candle closes after the news is out. We always let the wind blow "though the chimes first," so to speak, before we decide what to wear that day. And the good thing about the major economic releases is that they are scheduled ahead of time, so we know exactly when the wind will blow—we just don't know what direction it will come from. While there are billions of dollars in the accounts of investment banks and prop shop traders who react just milliseconds after the news, discretionary traders, or retail traders like us, are purposely removed from the actual event. We should react to where price ends up shortly after the news release, not to the release itself.

Some of the nuances we have just covered are not easy to demonstrate outside of a live trading environment. Because of this, we always extend an invitation to our clients to attend our Live Market Exercise at www.clovernest.com, which is complimentary, where Jay Norris points out trade setups and signals in live markets during the London and U.S. sessions. As you can imagine, the live market environment is much more conducive to demonstrating trading techniques than a text. The key is always being able to identify the current market price pattern, always knowing when risk is imminent (economic releases are scheduled well ahead of time), and knowing how to gauge when risk is increasing and decreasing.

Leading Indicator Markets

The two markets that have earned leading indicator status, in our experience, are the U.S. stock and bond markets. Both markets give us a good indication of whether risk in the marketplace is increasing or decreasing. A note of caution, however, when looking at "leading indicator markets": relationships change by definition, and just because a market has a strong correlation with another market or a group of markets one year does not mean that it will maintain that relationship the following year. It is always best to take a trade signal in a market because it gave a specific trigger and is in line with price pattern and risk. We don't teach parallel analysis (comparing direction between different markets to obtain a trading edge) because relationships by nature change, but individual market behavior, such as a trendline break and change of direction, tends to stay constant. There are securities markets, however, that do tend to telegraph risk more quickly, particularly during times of economic uncertainty.

In Exhibit 5-14, we have an hourly chart of the S&P 500 stock index, which represents the U.S. stock market, in the top panel, and an hourly chart of the EUR-USD in the bottom panel. The S&P 500,

Exhibit 5-14
Source: www.esignal.com.

more commonly called the Spoos, is an asset-class market (a blue chip, dividend-yielding stock index) and is considered a great proxy for the global economy, while the euro enjoys a correlation with asset-class markets because EUR-USD longs earn a slight interest rate and the euro is arguably considered a reserve currency in some countries. While the euro is not technically an asset-class market, it does currently (2010) enjoy a correlation with asset-class markets. If the Spoos are moving higher, it is a positive economic event and reflects a decreasing risk level in the markets. We have circled buy signals at the same time on both charts. Both markets rallied, but we can see the pronounced difference in behavior between the two.

While both markets ended up higher, it was a much smoother trip for the Spoos. The EUR-USD showed serious indecision (that is, higher risk) along the way, while the Spoos, true to form as a leading indicator market, showed little indecision (that is, low risk) as they consolidated the gains of the December 1, 2010, rally by moving sideways overnight and then resumed the up move on December 2, 2010. Also notice on the left side of the chart how the Spoos bottomed first on November 29, 2010, and then posted two slightly higher lows before rallying, while the EUR-USD didn't bottom until November 30, 2010. Leading indicator markets tend to discount risk more quickly and lead other markets during times of indecision while exhibiting more manageable risk. You do need to know that you would never take a trade in one market based on behavior in another market without a proper trigger occurring in line with the price pattern and knowledge of the economic calendar (incoming risk).

The U.S. Treasury bond market is still considered a flight to quality market, meaning that in times of economic uncertainty, money still flows into Treasuries at the expense of other asset-class markets. It can be said that if Treasury prices are moving higher, the risk for asset-class markets is increasing. In the chart in Exhibit 5-15, we have the U.S. 30-year Treasury bond in the bottom panel and AUD-USD in the top panel. The Aussie dollar is an asset-class market because holders earn interest on the currency, and the country enjoys very favorable long-term demographics and has a number of valuable natural resources. We can see how in the spring of 2010, a rally in Treasuries stopped a rally in the AUD-USD, causing a sharp correction. A sell-off in Treasuries means higher U.S. interest rates, which is bullish for the U.S. dollar. In times of economic uncertainty, higher bond prices also spell higher risk in the marketplace and are bearish for asset-class markets like the AUD-USD and global stock markets.

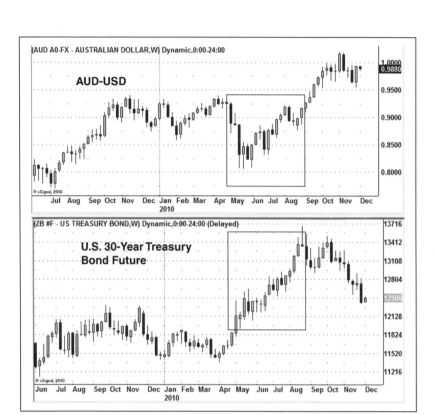

Exhibit 5-15
Source: www.esignal.com.

Once the rally in the bonds kicked off, the AUD-USD broke sharply, and the currency rally was put on hold until the fall. It's difficult for asset markets to move higher if U.S. Treasuries are also moving higher.

The most important thing to know about market fundamentals is that news = risk. It is either higher risk, no risk, or something in between. While there may be market participants who are good enough to take an educated guess as to what the effects of an economic release on a market will be, we don't do this. We rely on price to interpret the information first, then gauge whether the information increased or decreased risk, and take only the trade signal that is in line with price pattern and risk.

Chapter 6

MARKET FRAMEWORK

E lliott wave theory provides an effective enough market framework that our old friend Bill Williams, the author of *Trading Chaos, 2nd edition* (Wiley, 2004), defined it as the market's underlying structure.

Elliott Wave Theory

Bill has traded for more than 40 years and also has a Ph.D. in the behavioral sciences. Paul Tudor Jones, one of the best traders of our time, refers to the newsletter *Elliott Wave Theory* as one of the "four bibles of the business." Given the high opinion that such accomplished traders hold of the Elliott wave, it would be hard to close our minds to the potential of R. N. Elliott's works on market movement. What impresses us about the theory is seeing firsthand how often market movement unfolds in the same, or very similar, wave and channel patterns that were first described by Elliott so many years ago, and second, how it dovetails so well with other technical analysis studies and Dow theory in particular. The trader Cynthia Kase summed it up best in her book *Trading with the Odds* (McGraw-Hill, 1996): "Elliott's theories about the market in general and his view that there is a natural law that governs the market, are correct in broad terms."

The Elliott wave principle is primarily a trend-following school of technical analysis that describes market movements as waves. In Elliot wave theory, each market movement or wave pattern is designated with a numeric label (1 through 5) or a lettered label (A through C) and a behavioral designation — impulsive (trending) or reactive (corrective). It is named after the famed market analyst R. N. Elliott, who published his works in two notable books: *The Wave Principle* (1938) and *Nature's Laws: The Secret of the Universe* (1946). He wrote that a market movement, be it a bull move or a bear move, would be made up of eight separate waves, with the first five waves broken down into an impulsive wave (designated 1) followed by a corrective wave (designated 2), then another impulse wave (designated 3), followed by another corrective wave (designated 4), and then one more impulsive wave (designated 5). Wave 3 could not be the shortest and was often the longest pricewise, and Wave 4 was often the most complex.

This initial five-wave pattern would be followed by a three-wave corrective pattern labeled A, B, and C, with A and C being impulsive and B being reactive or corrective. The trending waves themselves could be broken down into five smaller waves with the same sequence as the overall move, while the corrective waves often fulfilled predictable retracements and broke down into three waves, two impulsive separated by one corrective. An example of this pattern can be seen in the daily EUR-USD chart in Exhibit 6-1.

Elliott believed that the Fibonacci summation series was the basis of his wave pattern. He theorized that it was crowd psychology that moved the markets, and that since this was the collective actions of individuals, and since those individuals, like all living things, were rhythmical, their actions could be predicted. He also proposed that there were waves within waves, with each smaller time frame mimicking the larger formation, a phenomenon that we now know to be fractal geometry.

We are by no means Elliotticians, or experts on Elliott wave theory. We are traders who have seen the familiar five-wave pattern unfold in too many markets over many years to not believe that there is something

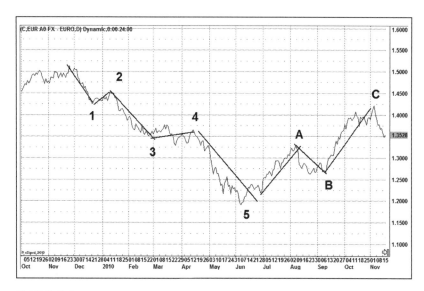

Exhibit 6-1
Source: www.esignal.com.

here that can help a trader if she is going along with the flow of the market and that same flow is unfolding in the predictable manner that Elliott, and now Prechter and others, teaches. Prechter's work in analyzing markets and categorizing how corrections unfold and eventually lead to impulsive, trending behavior, and how channel lines provide key structure in a market, are just as pertinent now as they were 30 years ago when he wrote his first book.

In the case of the Elliott wave theory, however, we do feel that less is more, and that you definitely need to keep it simple. The downside of the theory for many analysts and aspiring traders is that they take it too seriously and get lured down the "rabbit hole" of trying to account for every zig and zag on the intraday charts. There is an abundance of Elliott analysts on the Web today whose charts look like spider webs, with numbers and letters splattered on them like so many flies, and whose analysis does not include directional road signs and basic strength or weakness (momentum) readings. You don't ever want to

initiate a trade based on a wave pattern alone. Before you can understand
the flow of the market, you need to be able to define the specific directional determinants that highlight short-term trend shifts and provide
buy and sell signals, and know when those signals are in line with the
higher-time-frame price pattern.

The Elliott Wave Trade Is Subjective

The most important things to know about the Elliot wave are that it
is not a trading method in that it does not supply trading setups and
signals and trade management techniques, and that it does rely on an
individual's interpretation of it. While many analysts might call this
subjectivity a weakness, we see it as a plus, and we see the need to
always have an alternative wave count as a strength. Most traders'
weakness is one that they don't know they have, and that is the inability
to see both sides of the market. Once they get an opinion on direction, they become attached to trading only that side of the market.
Objectivity and the ability to understand the necessity of trading both
long and short in a market are qualities that serve traders well. There
are plenty of times that our opinions will be wrong, and we need to
know ahead of time that we will be better served by taking sell signals
in a market that we "thought" should go higher, or by taking buy signals
in a market that we "thought" should be going lower. Most trader
wannabes can't shift gears like this because they are still focusing on
their initial analysis. Our only goal is to follow our trading plan.

The Elliott wave is used for forecasting, while the trading method
in this book is designed for pinpointing setups and signals. We feel
strongly that if the inexperienced analyst or trader tries to study Elliott
wave theory first, before studying and understanding the foundation
of trading, which is identifying obvious price patterns, being able to
measure momentum, definitively measuring price direction, and
understanding the importance of chart structure (support and resistance), it will only cause confusion. You also need to understand that

Elliott wave theory is going to work best on higher time frames, such as weekly, daily, or hourly charts, and that the further down the scale you go, from higher time frames to lower time frames, the more complicated the patterns become, and therefore the more risky they are for the trader.

It is human nature to think that you can find the easiest, fastest road to success, and trading lower time frames is a potent lure, but you have to realize that while markets can move fast, this is not the norm, and large price shifts take time to build and backfill. There are plenty of traders who were right on the long-term trend but got crushed when a lower-time-frame, low-volume retracement extended itself beyond the 50 percent norm. If you choose to study Elliot wave theory to improve your trading, remember to focus on the higher-time-frame charts and understand that price direction and momentum are still the keys to trade selection and management.

Corrections Following Waves

Elliott's original works, and those of Robert Prechter, remain, in our opinion, some of the most definitive works available on how markets move. From our perspective, however, you will need to get over the temptation of trying to predict market movement and not try to categorize every movement in every market, but learn from the many real-time examples in today's markets of how reactive, corrective price action shifts to impulsive, trending price behavior, and how channel lines often provide important structure, as the hourly chart in Exhibit 6-2 demonstrates.

One of the most widely heeded of Elliott's contributions by experienced traders is his categorizing of waves (price movements), and Wave 3 in particular. The rule for Wave 3 is that it cannot be the shortest wave, and most often it is the longest wave. Because it is often the longest wave, for many traders, catching a Wave 3 is the most desirable trade

Exhibit 6-2
Source: www.esignal.com.

they can make. The Wave 3 is also the second impulsive (think trending) wave in a market movement, and it stands to reason that the odds of catching a second impulsive wave would be better than those of catching the first or third impulsive wave. The first impulsive wave can't be identified as impulsive until it is already underway, and the third impulsive move (Wave 5 for Elliotticians) would be the trickiest because of the complex correction following Wave 3. Simply put, for a trader, the odds on identifying a second impulsive price move following the first one are better than those for identifying that initial move or a third move, particularly if you do not handcuff yourself with too many theories and rules and focus on taking advantage of the fact that markets move up and down.

Exhibit 6-3 provides a good example of a Wave 3 in the EUR-USD on an intraday chart that spans the Tokyo/London overlap through the London/U.S. overlap. Wave 1 crests right at the London open—8 a.m. GMT, 2 a.m. CDT—and corrects lower. At this point, we don't know

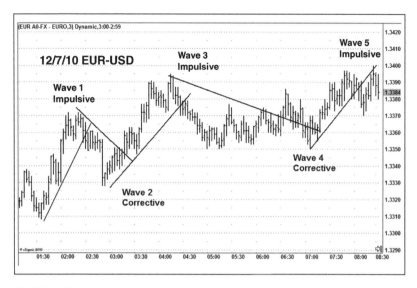

Exhibit 6-3
Source: www.esignal.com.

that the up move is a Wave 1; we just know it was impulsive. What we do know is that impulsive price movement is going to be followed by reactive, or corrective, price movement, which in turn will be followed by impulsive price movement again.

Once price starts to correct lower, retracing the impulse rally, we draw a bear trendline from the top of Wave 1, bordering the high points of the correction (Wave 2), with the idea that when the correction runs its course and price closes above the trendline (resistance line), we will see another impulsive rally. Given that the market has already rallied once and then corrected, it becomes more likely that a second rally, or a Wave 3, will ensue, which it does at approximately 3:15 a.m. CDT, 9:15 a.m. GMT.

Another valuable tool that Elliott highlighted in his works is his observations of retracements (corrections) following impulsive price moves and how they often end at predictable levels. The most written about of these "Fibonacci levels" are the 0.382 level, the 50 percent

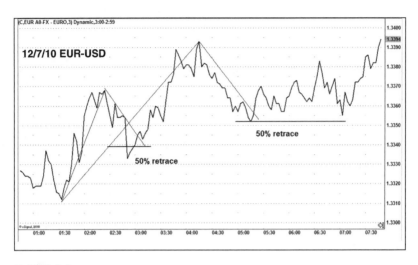

Exhibit 6-4
Source: www.esignal.com.

level, and the 0.618 level. Professional traders won't split hairs on exact levels for sure, although it makes for great examples when a market stops at an exact level after the fact, but the most useful level that we have seen, year in, year out, on all time-frame charts is the 50 percent level. Time and time again, we see price corrections stop right around the 50 percent level, change direction, and revert back to impulsive price movement. In Exhibit 6-4, we've taken the same chart as in Exhibit 6-3 and marked the retracement levels.

Exhibit 6-5 depicts another example of 50 percent retracements in the EUR-USD in 2010, this time on the daily chart.

One of the few guarantees in trading is that markets move up and down. Knowing that markets retrace themselves following trend moves is noteworthy. Knowing that these retracements often stop near predetermined levels based on a predictable percentage of the most recent impulsive move should lend us confidence, which is where Elliott wave analysis comes in. Waiting for price to react to these levels with a change of direction and a trendline break, however, takes

Exhibit 6-5
Source: www.esignal.com.

patience, while actually entering a trade and managing that trade takes discipline.

We don't teach Elliott wave theory in our courses because it is analysis, and we focus more on trade selection and management, but we recommend Prechter's first book, *Elliott Wave Principle*, which he wrote with Alfred Frost in 1978, as a starting point to learn the basics of this interesting and highly regarded market theory.

PART TWO

Trading

Chapter 7

TRADE SETUP

The overview defines the short-term trends for a market's different time frames (price pattern) and identifies any confluence of support or resistance on the chart (structure), along with identifying momentum. The "setup" defines the point in the current trend where a potential change of direction could occur, with a change of direction being defined as a close beyond a directional line. Wherever you have a directional line, you have a potential setup in the making. A trend always starts with a change of direction and always ends with a change of direction. It is the point in the current trend that separates the current direction and a change of direction that we call a "setup." This is why the highest closing candles and lowest closing candles in trends are so important to us, because they are potential trade setups.

The low of the highest closing candle of the current move or the high of the lowest closing candle of the current move, when combined with a trendline, defines that point in both price and time where the setup ends and a signal (trigger) is given that marks the beginning of a new trend. While the terms *setup* and *current trend* are very closely related, because a setup is essentially the potential end of the current trend and the beginning of a new trend, it is those highest closing candles and lowest closing candles at the end of a trend, or setup candles, that help pinpoint the price point that determines whether we take action. You want to start seeing these candles on the chart along with the accompanying trendlines and understanding that these are

Exhibit 7-1
Source: www.esignal.com.

pivotal areas at which price can and often will change its direction. Exhibit 7-1 provides an excellent example.

You also need to start understanding that price movement is never predetermined to the degree that most people think it is; there is never a guarantee that price will or won't move in a certain direction.

When price is approaching a level marked by the confluence of a directional line and a trendline, you need to maintain a relaxed yet focused state. And you always need to remember that a market's price can go either up or down, and your job isn't to anticipate which way price is going to move; it's to follow your plan and enter a trade only when you get a signal that fits the specific criteria spelled out in your trading plan. For us, that means taking trades only when structure and momentum are complementing the price pattern.

Structure will also play a key role in your setup. It can be said that structure will often cradle the setup, then shift in support of the trade for those times when the market follows through in the direction of the setup and signal. When we refer to structure shifting, we are referring to when the pivot points reset themselves at the close of the day, week, or month, or when a new trendline or retracement is created by a higher low or a lower high. Very often it is chart structure that provides the framework of the setup, with a trendline or pivot point or retracement level providing the level that price holds prior to setting itself up for a trade.

It's important to know that structure is factual, meaning that it is clearly defined in price and time. The exception to this would be trendlines, to a degree, although there is no disputing the slope of a line connecting two points. The subjectivity comes from which trendlines to rely on. In a trending market, one in which the higher time frames are coordinated, we want to rely on looser trendlines drawn from the actual highs and lows of candles, allowing the market room to breathe. In contrast, in countertrending markets (that is, markets in which the different time frames are in flux), we need to draw trendlines from the bodies of the candles, so that we can classify price shifts more quickly and get into trades sooner when the intermediate-term or long-term direction reasserts itself.

The example in Exhibit 7-2 shows a trend shift on a 240-minute chart with a box that highlights the time period depicted on a lower-time-frame chart in Exhibit 7-3. We see a trend shift at the beginning of a new week, which coincided with a shift in the weekly pivot points. (Pivot points readjust themselves on the close of the last candle of the day for a daily pivot, on the close of the last candle of the week for the weekly pivots, and so on.) Price then falls below the weekly central pivot in our example and posts a lower low than the last low of the previous uptrend, before turning higher at weekly S1. The lower low is significant because at that point, we can say that the price pattern has changed from bullish to bearish. Price then produces a countertrend rally from weekly S1 up to the central pivot point, which we mark with a body-to-body bull trendline. This two-candle rally proves to be the first lower high in a new downtrend.

Exhibit 7-2
Source: www.esignal.com.

We've also highlighted August 11, 2010 with a box; broken down that day further by giving a 15-minute chart from that same day with daily pivots in Exhibit 7-3; and marked the setups on this chart in line with the higher-time-frame chart.

On the 15-minute chart in Exhibit 7-3, we can see the advantage of identifying setups that are in line with the long-term trend. After all, the long-term trend on the 15-minute chart is equal to the short-term trend on the 240-minute chart. And as we explained in Chapter 3, it's much easier to determine the short-term trend on a higher-time-frame chart using the trendline and the directional line than it is to determine the long-term trend on a lower-time-frame chart. We also want you to notice in Exhibit 7-3 how all three of the setups circled concluded with a change-of-direction candle. A change-of-direction candle is a candle that closes beyond and shifts the directional line.

Exhibit 7-3
Source: www.esignal.com.

Exhibits 7-2 and 7-3 both epitomize how we use price pattern and structure to identify attractive setups. We can see on the 240-minute chart in Exhibit 7-2 how the price pattern shifted from exhibiting higher lows and higher highs above its weekly pivot points to showing lower lows and lower highs beneath its weekly pivot points. The pivots are aligned with price pattern—structure is complementing price. Once we see that direction is defined and being supported by structure, we can drop down to the lower-time-frame chart (in this example, the 15-minute chart) and wait for setups on that time frame that are in agreement with price pattern, structure, and the higher-time-frame trend.

As we said before, every trendline and every directional line is a potential setup. When we stop and think about that, it's telling us that there are going to be setups quite often because as price moves through time, it is going to be constantly creating and recreating trends and directional lines. Once we understand this continuous process of old trends giving way and new trends forming, we start to see why market direction causes so much confusion and causes so many people to lose their money. Based on this continual motion of impulsive price action followed by reactive price action (trending movement followed by corrective movement), the trader is going to have to make a new decision every time the market gives a new setup.

We know from stress tests that the more decisions an individual has to make, the greater the likelihood that the individual will make a mistake. Add in a time element by speeding up the questions (decision points), and the average individual will move from being correct the majority of the time to being correct less and less, until you reach a speed at which the majority of his decisions are wrong. Welcome to the world of day trading. The way to avoid this mental treadmill is to know how to focus on those price setups that are in line with the higher-time-frame trends. To do this takes more than knowing how to update structure; it takes a specific mindset that is geared toward avoiding distraction, understanding the risks you're taking, and being able to follow very specific orders without question. This combination in individuals is rare, and it is definitely not a natural combination. The good news is that it is learned behavior.

The trickiest part of that combination is being a risk taker. Many individuals who have the knowledge to recognize what and where to focus on and the patience to wait for those conditions to set up just don't have the conviction to pull the trigger when it comes time for them to risk their money and take the trade. This is generally because they do not believe that what they are doing will be profitable, since they don't yet have the experience of seeing it be profitable. If you have the knowledge, patience, and a thorough understanding of risk based on extensive back-testing of the method you use to trade (that is, the experience), then trading is very often

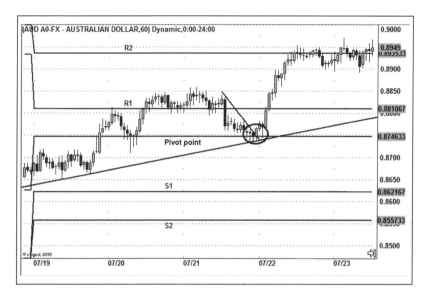

Exhibit 7-4
Source: www.esignal.com.

just a matter of being in the right place at the right time. A good
example of being in the right place at the right time is the snapshot
of a 60-minute chart of AUD-USD with weekly pivot points and
trendlines overlaid in Exhibit 7-4.

Trade setups don't get much more pristine than this buy setup and
signal on July 22, 2010 in AUD-USD just ahead of the London open.
The central pivot and a long-term trendline create a confluence of
support that first cradles price, then provides a powerful buy setup that
launches price a full 200 pips higher. Given the trendline in place
starting on the left side of the chart, which marks the pattern of higher
lows, there is no need even for a higher-time-frame chart to confirm
direction. The confluence of the trendline and the weekly central
pivot provides the confirmation that we need. The most important
thing about this trade setup is how the overall price pattern is being
complemented by the pivot points.

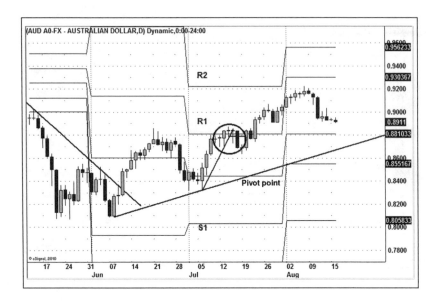

Exhibit 7-5
Source: www.esignal.com.

The next example, in Exhibit 7-5, is a sell setup that did not work. It had both a trendline and a directional-line shift, both of which occurred on pivot R1 and culminated with a change-of-direction candle that closed below R1. One reason the setup was questionable from the start is price pattern; there was already a higher low in place from the previous month's low. And R2 did not provide resistance as much as it provided a "rest stop" for price on the road higher. We can see this because price actually closed above the R1 level several times, and even made a higher high than the June high, before the change-of-direction candle.

These subtle occurrences are important in helping us to make a determination that the price pattern and structure do not support this setup, and in the weekly chart from this same time period, shown in Exhibit 7-6, we see that price was actually in the process of clearing higher-time-frame resistance when it gave this small correction on the

Exhibit 7-6
Source: www.esignal.com.

daily chart, which indicates that neither price pattern nor structure was confirming. We can say with assurance that the setup on the daily chart does not have structure supporting price pattern in the direction of the trade.

The change-of-direction candle on the daily chart was just a correction following an impulsive move, not a reversal, while Exhibit 7-6 provides evidence that higher time structure and momentum did not support that sell setup, based on the bullish benchmark candle that occurred on this weekly chart just before the circled candle. There is no doubt that this was not an easy example to analyze. Because of the questions raised, however, we should have been able to determine that it was not a high-probability setup, which points out the wisdom of seeking out only those setups where it is obvious that we have price pattern, structure, and momentum in our favor. In other words, be patient enough to wait for those pristine setups where it is obvious that we have everything on the chart lined up in our favor.

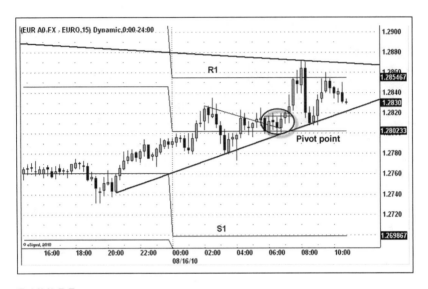

Exhibit 7-7
Source: www.esignal.com.

Ideally, we have also made the point that you need to know what is occurring on the higher-time-frame charts and that you always need to be updating your trendlines. Exhibit 7-7, a 15-minute EUR-USD chart with daily pivots overlaid, provides a great reminder of this. We get a pristine setup right at the intersection of the central pivot and a body-to-body trendline (it is a body-to-body trendline because the move it is marking is a countertrend move on the higher-time-frame charts). The way to have maximized our performance using this buy setup would have been to have drawn the higher-time-frame trendline ahead of time, and been quick enough to exit the long trade at that trendline just above pivot R1 because we understood that while the setup was for a trend trade on the 15-minute chart, it was still a countertrend trade on the four-hour and daily charts. This figure also highlights why we need to know the market's stance on its various time frames so that we are always in a position to make real-time decisions using structure and price pattern.

Once we see price get rejected by the trendline, and we know that we are trading counter to the higher time frames, we need to react quickly to protect our position and our account. If we were basing our trading decisions only off the 15-minute chart, we would have seen our profits wiped out very quickly and possibly even have taken a loss on the trade. By having that longer-term trendline drawn ahead of time, however, we would have known not only that we were in a countertrend trade, but that we would need to sell at least a portion of our position, if not all of it, on that structure or consider tightening up stops on the balance of our position (more on this in Chapter 9).

We need to be aware of the directional lines as structure also. In Exhibit 7-8, an S&P 500 futures 15-minute chart, we have a rally on the lower-time-frame chart that stalls at the confluence of its daily directional line and daily pivot resistance 1. The stall isn't as important as what happened next. We get a close below the intermediate-term

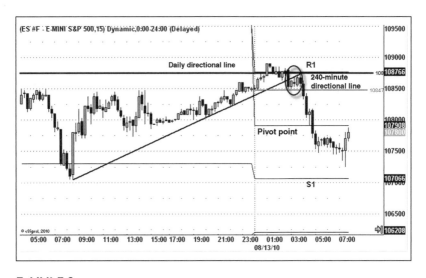

Exhibit 7-8
Source: www.esignal.com.

trendline to change price direction, followed by a small bear flag, then a close below the 240-minute directional line, and the market plummets. Setups that occur at or on a confluence of structure are always worth monitoring.

The key to being in a position to take advantage of these setups is to be at your work space on time, every day, with an open mind, having already drawn your trendlines and directional lines and having the appropriate pivot points in place. A strong work ethic and a belief that you are a professional trader will go a long way. There will always be risks in trading, and you will have losers, but if you show up every day with the right mindset and execute only trades that are in accordance with your trading plan, then you will be in a better position to put trades like the one highlighted in Exhibit 7-8 into your account.

In Chapter 2, we talked about the difficulty of trading during July and August, when many of the more experienced and better-capitalized traders are on holiday and volume is low, so that price action becomes much "jumpier." The daily EUR-USD chart in Exhibit 7-9 epitomizes this.

What will keep you out of trouble in such a market if you are an end-of-day trader is recognizing how structure is supporting the overall pattern, and focusing only on setups in that same direction. In mid-July, we have a setup candle circled that was also a change-of-direction candle that closed below the central pivot. Inexperienced traders would take this as a sign of weakness in the market and point out how the short-term trend has shifted lower. However, by focusing on the trendline connecting the June and July lows, and marking the weekly directional line, we would know that the intermediate-term trend for EUR-USD remained higher, which would have kept us focused on buy setups. While trading remained choppy through the end of August—similar to the price pattern in late July—the intermediate-term trend held higher, and the buy setup

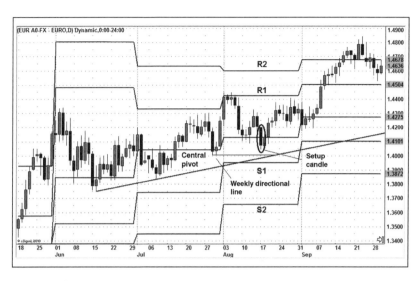

Exhibit 7-9
Source: www.esignal.com.

created by the lowest closing candle in mid-July (circled) proved a nice trend trade.

Exhibit 7-10 highlights another trade setup that occurred during the dog days of August 2009. The long-term trend was lower, yet USD-JPY gave us a summer soda-pop rally that ended in an exhaustive momentum and a setup candle in the first week of that month. The term *soda-pop rally* comes from comparing a market move to what happens if someone shakes up a bottle of carbonated soda pop before giving it to you—when you uncap the bottle, the liquid shoots out all at once, making a mess, and it's over before you've figured out what happened. This summer "pop" was strong enough to shift the intermediate-term trend higher and even took out the previous month's high, but it ran out of "fizz" as the long-term trend exerted itself. By marking the low of this highest closing candle, we gave ourselves that all-important point in price that we knew price would have to close beyond to reverse the uptrend. And once price did close below that

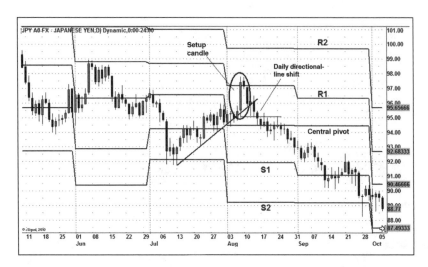

Exhibit 7-10
Source: www.esignal.com.

level, the market went into the type of steady price move that currency markets are known for. This chart also highlights the importance of R1 as resistance in a long-term downtrend.

One of the most important questions to ask yourself, and one that you need to be asking often, is, "What's the setup?" The answer to this question is going to come more easily if you've done a proper overview and you have your trendlines and pivot points in place. By focusing in, identifying the current trend and when and where it started, and identifying the previous setup, we are going to put ourselves in a good position to monitor the current trend and identify the setup to catch the next trade. This is why it is so important for you to be on the screen when you are supposed to be there and to have updated all your trendlines and potential retracements ahead of time so that you can update your spreadsheet where you keep all this valuable information.

In Chapter 2, we talked about work ethic. We made the comparison to a business owner, and we made the point that if you are a business owner, you had better understand that you must show up prepared and on time. It is crucial that you understand that as a professional trader, you are no different from any business owner. You will be much more adept at spotting setups if you arrive at your work-station a little earlier than usual, and if you are mentally prepared before you make any analytic decisions. For further examples of trade setups on color charts, go to trading-u.com/tradeselection.asp.

Chapter 8

TRIGGER DEFINED
AND TRADE ENTERED

O nce you know how to conduct a proper overview and identify a trade setup, the most important thing we can teach you as a trader is to take fact-based triggers. A fact-based trigger is one where price fulfills specific conditions at the close of the candle or bar. This is very important because changing price conditions over the life of a candle will affect the technical indicators; for example, as price moves up and down, moving averages can cross and uncross, or the MACD can show momentum and then go flat. Basing decisions on a closed candle also shows you that price actually closed beyond structure and didn't just flirt with it. By taking a reading only at the close of the candle, when the indicators close also and price is either above or below structure, we lessen our chances of taking false signals.

We also always want the fact-based trigger to be complemented by support or resistance levels and supported by momentum. And then we need to err on the side of letting a profit run. Trendlines, pivot points, retracements, and weekly and monthly highs and lows are the most important support or resistance levels on the chart, and you need to make sure that price closes beyond these levels before committing to a trade. Likewise, you need to watch the MACD, or whatever centered oscillator you follow, and determine what it is telling you about current momentum. You are also going to need to understand up front that you will have losers, and that how you let them affect you will determine your success.

In our text *Mastering the Currency Market* (McGraw-Hill, 2009), we introduced you to the essential trading concepts that will provide the building blocks for your trading plan. It's time now to get more specific and show you how to trade in any market, on any time frame. Before you move forward, it would be an excellent idea for you to go back and review Chapters 5 and 10 of *Mastering the Currency Market*, where we introduce the concepts of using the behavior of individual candles, trendlines, and technical indicators to provide trade signals.

The single biggest problem for beginning traders, and the main reason why such a high percentage of speculators lose, is that they don't understand what their job is. They think their goal is to figure out which way the market is going to move next. They get attached to an opinion on which way a market is going to move, and they can't react when price does something different from their expectation. Most speculators spend too much time reading news stories to justify their opinion on market direction, instead of just going along with where a market goes.

The discretionary trader's only goal should be to follow her trading plan and avoid errors. Any action taken that is not in the trading plan is an error. By learning how to recognize a market's current pattern of highs and lows and definitively measure price direction on any time frame, and by using chart structure (support and resistance) to complement current price direction and momentum for timing, you are going to avoid the distraction and mental pitfall of thinking about what price is going to do next. This will make it much easier for you to take the trade trigger and initiate a position in a market when the time comes.

Before we define the trigger we are going to be using, we need to review what we call a change-of-direction candle. A change-of-direction

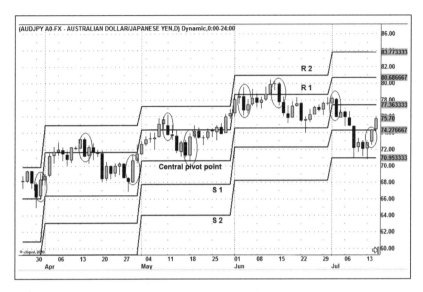

Exhibit 8-1
Source: www.esignal.com.

candle is any candle that closes beyond and shifts a directional line. The directional line is again defined as the horizontal line that marks the low of the highest closing candle in an uptrend, or that marks the high of the lowest closing candle in a downtrend. The close of the change-of-direction candle is a significant occurrence in time because it can provide one of the first signs that a trend may be coming to an end. In Exhibit 8-1, we've circled some of the more influential change-of-direction candles.

We often see change-of-direction candles before even leading indicators like the stochastic record a slowing of momentum. This does not mean that you take a change-of-direction candle as a signal. However, it is one of three possible variables that mark the trigger we are going to be using. If the close of the change-of-direction candle is not a trigger in itself, it is often a street sign on the road that leads you to the trigger. The other two variables are trendline shifts on a closing basis of the short-term trendline and/or the intermediate-term trendline.

When price simultaneously closes beyond both a trendline and a directional line, this is a trigger, or trade signal. When a trade signal occurs that is in line with the long-term price pattern and is supported by the current price structure (pivot points, retracements, and other trendlines), it is all the more attractive. This is what we mean when we say that structure must complement price pattern before we take a trade. This does not mean that we must always trade in the same direction as the long-term trend. Countertrend moves are a part of price movement, and by limiting ourselves to only taking trend trades, we would be taking ourselves out of the "flow" of taking both trend and countertrend signals and managing trades. The key to having the freedom to take countertrend signals is that you are well versed in distinguishing trend signals from countertrend signals.

Notice in Exhibit 8-1 how price reacted following each change-of-direction candle, and notice the connection between which side of a pivot that change-of-direction candle pointed to and which way price moved afterwards. (Also notice how well placing your stop loss order above the high of the bearish change-of-direction candle or below the low of the bullish change-of-direction candle would have worked. We will cover this topic in more detail in Chapter 9.) On only one of these circled candles did price not follow through in the direction it was pointed in following that change of direction.

Change-of-direction candles are a very important component of a trade signal for us. They are the first indication that the current trend is more likely to be ending, and that we should look for signs of sideways price action, or possibly even a reversal. The most functional trigger we can teach you is the combination of a trendline break on a closing basis and a change-of-direction candle. This versatile trigger becomes more reliable when there is higher-time-frame confirmation, or when the momentum is strong enough to give us simultaneous directional-line shifts such as we see in Exhibit 8-2, where the one day's price action took price beyond both its daily and its weekly directional lines.

(ZC #F - CORN,D) Dynamic,0:00-24:00 (Delayed)

Buy signal in corn with price closing above its trendline and both its weekly and daily directional lines

Trendline

Weekly directional line

Daily directional line

Exhibit 8-2
Source: www.esignal.com.

In *Mastering the Currency Market*, we taught you how to use a trendline breach on a closing basis and a stochastic cross to identify trade triggers. Now we've taught you the importance of the directional lines. We still use the stochastic and the trendline to identify signals, along with the directional line; however, we now do not need to wait for the stochastic to cross through its overbought or oversold levels before declaring a trigger. The chart of Apple (AAPL) in Exhibit 8-3 provides a good example of using this technique to exit long positions or even short the stock following rallies.

Trend and Countertrend Triggers

There are five types of entry signals that we will cover here. Two are trend triggers, and three are countertrend triggers.

- *Trend 1.* Trendline penetration on a closing basis and change of direction and stochastic cross with higher-time-frame confirmation.

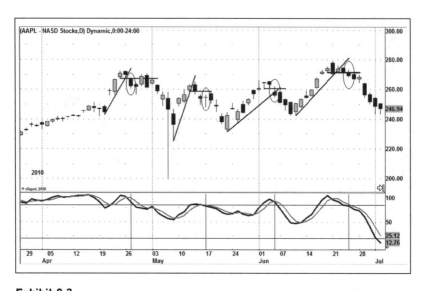

Exhibit 8-3
Source: www.esignal.com.

> (Higher-time-frame confirmation means that direction on the higher-time-frame chart is in agreement with the short-term trendline and directional line.)
>
> - *Trend 2.* Trendline penetration on a closing basis and change of direction and stochastic cross with no higher-time-frame confirmation, but on or above the long-term or intermediate-term bull trendline for a buy (or on or below the long-term or intermediate-term bear trendline for a sell) or on a significant higher-time-frame retracement level.
> - *Countertrend 1.* Trendline penetration on a closing basis and stochastic cross, and/or change of direction on a lower time frame, following supportive candle behavior on a higher time frame.
> - *Countertrend 2.* Trendline break on a closing basis, on significant support or resistance, with no higher-time-frame confirmation.
> - *Countertrend 3.* Close beyond high or low of doji on support or resistance with no change of direction or trendline break (A doji is a price candle where the opening and closing prices are very close to each other indicating price decision.)

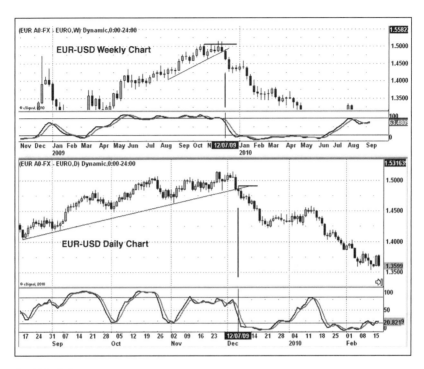

Exhibit 8-4
Source: www.esignal.com.

The chart in Exhibit 8-4 depicts a Trend 1 setup and trade, which is a trendline penetration on a closing basis and a change of direction and stochastic cross on the lower time frame, in this case the daily chart, with higher-time-frame confirmation on the weekly chart. In Exhibit 8-5, we have an example of a Trend 2 signal with a short-term trendline penetration on a closing basis and a change of direction and stochastic cross with no higher-time-frame confirmation, but just below a 50 percent retracement level of the 2007–2008 sell off.

This is a case in which the primary trend that started in 2007—the long-term trend—remained down, but the short-term trend had turned higher on both the weekly and the monthly charts. If we wait for the monthly chart to shift lower before taking a sell signal on the weekly

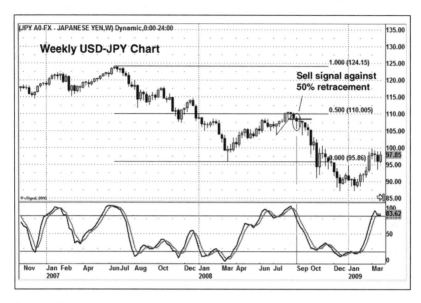

Exhibit 8-5
Source: www.esignal.com.

chart, we risk missing a large move. Given that price had retraced less than 66 percent of the previous down—move, we can consider that move to still be intact and consider a trade signal on a significant retracement level such as 50 percent to be a trend trade, particularly if there is a confluence of structure such as a higher-time-frame pivot point. Students of Dow theory believe that a primary trend can retrace up to 66 percent of itself and still remain intact.

We define a trend trade as a trade taken in the same direction as the higher-time-frame trends. Trend trades are desirable because they are simpler to manage, meaning that there are fewer decisions to make, and thus fewer possible mistakes to make, and they have a higher risk/reward ratio. Many beginning traders shy away from trend trading because they see only the higher-risk half of the risk/reward ratio. And they get lured into thinking that "if a market moves just a little bit, I can make good money," which leads them to countertrend trading. They don't understand that by focusing on "little moves," they risk going against the intermediate-term and long-term trends, which actually increases their risk because it lowers their winning percentage. Rather than be patient and put on a small position with the idea of leaving it on for many days, if not weeks or longer, they get lured into putting on multiple contracts over very short time periods, which leads to the micromanaging of trades and increases the number of decisions they must make, which increases the probability of their making errors. The most important thing you need to know about trend trading is how to measure the current direction of the short-term, intermediate-term, and long-term trends. Once you know this, you will by definition know not only when the market is trending, but when it is exhibiting countertrending behavior.

Exhibit 8-6 highlights a Countertrend 1 trigger in the AUD-USD in early 2009, which is trendline penetration on a closing basis and stochastic cross, and/or change of direction on a lower time frame, following supportive candle behavior on a higher time frame. In this case, we do not quite get a change of direction on the lower-time-frame daily chart, but we do have a short-term trendline break and a stochastic cross—remember that we need the trendline break, but the stochastic and change of direction occurrences are "and/or" conditions, meaning either/or, as long as there is supportive candle behavior on the higher time frame. The and/or condition is included to give us the freedom to get into a trade more quickly if higher-time-frame resistance and price create conditions that are supportive of the signal on the lower time frame, or if we see a price move culminate on exhaustive momentum, creating a very long setup candle, meaning that before a change of direction could occur, there would have to be a large percentage move in the opposite direction.

As with our signal in Trend 2, the primary, or long-term, trend on the higher-time-frame chart was lower in Exhibit 8-6; however, the short-term trend was higher, as was the intermediate-term trend on

Exhibit 8-6
Source: www.esignal.com.

the lower-time-frame daily chart. By heeding the shooting star on structure (pivot resistance 1) and taking the signal on the lower time frame, the trader assumes a more defined risk in that he can place his stop beyond the high of the move, which is two candles back from the signal candle. We will talk much more about trade and risk management in Chapter 9.

An example of a Countertrend 2 signal can be seen in the Dow Jones Industrial Average in Exhibit 8-7, as we have a trendline break on a closing basis, below significant resistance (the February 2008 high) in the lower panel, with no higher-time-frame confirmation on

Exhibit 8-7
Source: www.esignal.com.

the weekly chart in the top panel. We can see from the weekly chart on top that the stochastic is pointed up and that there is a clear pattern of higher lows and higher highs. Despite the sharp one-day sell-off highlighted on the daily chart, the sell trigger proved to be a loser, as the uptrend on the weekly chart held, and price recovered to make a higher monthly high later that same month.

Exhibit 8-8 highlights a Countertrend 3 signal, which in this case is a close beyond the low of a doji on pivot resistance 2. There is no change of direction or trendline break needed. This trigger would be appropriate to exit a trade or a portion of a trade to protect principal, but not necessarily to initiate a trade.

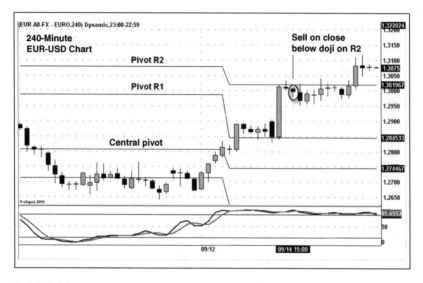

(EUR A0-FX - EURO,240) Dynamic,23:00-22:59

240-Minute
EUR-USD Chart

Sell on close
below doji on R2

Pivot R2

Pivot R1

Central pivot

09/12   09/14 15:00

Exhibit 8-8
Source: www.esignal.com.

A countertrending market is defined as one in which the direction on two or more time frames is counter to each other. Using a countertrend trigger, however, does not necessarily mean that you are taking a countertrend trade. You can use such a trigger to exit a trend trade or a portion of a trade to protect your account, or because you are uncomfortable with the possibility that the countertrend trade could end up reversing the intermediate or primary trend against you. There are times when you will want to enter a countertrend trade, such as when the current direction of the daily chart is opposite to that the four-hour chart or the direction of the four-hour chart is opposite to that of the one-hour chart. Given these situations where price is obviously not trending, you can take signals on the lower time frames without regard to higher-time-frame confirmation.

If you take a countertrend signal to initiate a trade, you need to know how to manage the position off the right side of the lower-time-frame chart, and you need to be mindful of short-term structure. As a rule of thumb, the longer you are in a countertrend trade, the riskier it becomes. You do not want to be in a position where time is not on your side and price is skittish on every bit of short-term structure. If you are in a countertrend trade, price does happen to move significantly in favor of your position, and the time frames coordinate and you get higher-time-frame confirmation on a closing basis (that is, the market starts to trend), you can then manage the trade off the higher-time-frame chart.

It's most important to understand that for countertrend trades — (trades where you do not have higher-time-frame confirmation), you need to get in quickly to improve your positioning, and exit quickly if you do not get follow-through. If you do not get an indication that the higher-time-frame confirmation is coming, you would exit on the first change of direction on the lower time frame. When you are countertrend trading, you will be better served by taking setups and signals on the lower time frames. Change of direction is very important to us as traders. However, there are two circumstances in which we will pass on a signal regardless of change of direction. Both are countertrend signals. Recognizing these circumstances will also help us to manage our trades better, and more specifically help us to let a profit run, as you see in Chapter 9.

Signals to Avoid

Our trade triggers are quite specific; however, you still need to make sure that the three criteria of price pattern, structure, and momentum are in place. The most commonly overlooked of these three necessities is momentum. This is because most momentum indicators are lagging indicators, and most account holders lack the patience, or the understanding, to use such an important component of trading to their advantage.

A signal can occur when there is no significant structure (support or resistance), and if momentum does not confirm, meaning that you do

Exhibit 8-9
Source: www.esignal.com.

not get a marked move in the MACD or other momentum indicators that you use, then this is generally going to be a retracement in a higher-time-frame trend, and thus a trade that you want to avoid. Exhibit 8-9 provides a good example of this. First we get a trade signal with an initial change of direction and a trendline break on June 15, with price following through on the next two candles, which is confirmed by the MACD indicator. Then the market upticks and gives us a change of direction (circled), but the retracement is less than 66 percent of the initial move and is not confirmed by momentum (the MACD). We would dismiss the circled signal because it did not trigger on or above support and was not confirmed by a technical indicator measuring momentum (in this case, the MACD). This is a signal where you may have had price pattern in support of the signal (the market was in an uptrend), but you did not have structure favoring it because the signal was occurring below that 66 percent retracement level, and you did not have momentum supporting the trade, as we can see that the MACD and its trigger line barely budged despite the short-term trendline breach and change of direction.

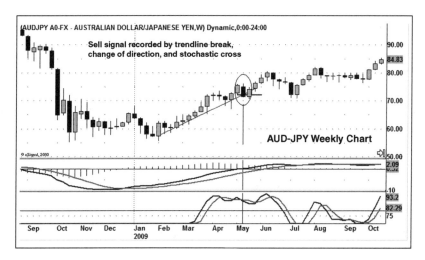

Exhibit 8-10
Source: www.esignal.com.

The fact that the signal in Exhibit 8-9 did not work reminds us of the importance of taking trade signals only where price pattern, structure, and momentum are aligned.

Exhibit 8-10 provides another example of a trade signal not to take.

If you have a change of direction and a stochastic cross in an extended uptrend that is not confirmed by momentum (meaning that you do not see a cross of the MACD and its trigger line) and the current pattern of higher highs and higher lows (or lower lows and lower highs) is not threatened, as seen in the example in Exhibit 8-10, you can dismiss the signal. Notice how the MACD in Exhibit 8-10 is showing the same angle throughout the move, with the black line parallel to the grey line, and despite the stochastic cross and change-of-direction candle, price does not break the pattern of higher highs and higher lows. This is telling us that despite price changing direction, momentum is still favoring a continuation of the intermediate-term up move.

Exhibit 8-11 is an example of price giving us all three conditions for a trigger, but the previous momentum on the upside held, and the

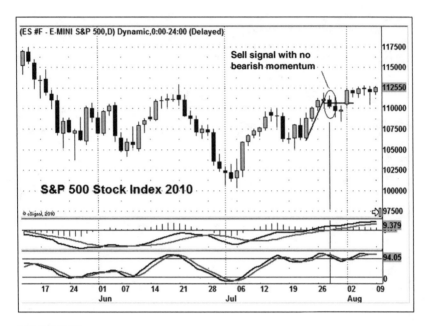

Exhibit 8-11
Source: www.esignal.com.

signal would have produced a losing trade. While price gave us a change of direction and a trendline break with a stochastic cross, it did not threaten the integrity of the pattern of higher lows, higher highs, and higher closes and momentum held, as recorded by the MACD, favoring a continuation of the move that was in place already, so we would pass on the signal.

There is a reason why we have covered trade signals this late in the text, and we hope you understand what that reason is. There is so much more to trading than entering and exiting trades.

Mastering Trade Selection

The key to trade selection is going to come down to always making sure that you are patient in waiting for a proper signal, and then taking

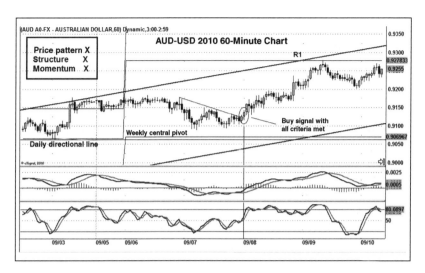

Exhibit 8-12
Source: www.esignal.com.

signals only when the three additional criteria of price pattern, structure, and momentum are in your favor.

Exhibit 8-12 highlights a signal using textbook trade selection criteria. The signal is not considered until there is a trendline break on a closing basis and a change of direction, with stochastic confirmation. Next, the trader needs to check off the three other conditions. Taking price pattern first, we can see from the diagonal channel lines that frame the overall price action that the primary or long-term trend is higher, as is the overall price pattern. Taking structure next, we can see that price is already above both its weekly central pivot and its daily directional line. We can now check off that we have both price pattern and structure in favor of a long signal. We look to our lagging momentum (the MACD), and we can see that on the close of the signal, candle momentum is accelerating, with the MACD pulling away from its trigger line.

It will be your job as a professional trader to wait for trade signals that have these favorable conditions in place before you risk your money or your clients' money in the market. By doing so, you are going to ensure that you will be trading not only with the current trend, but also with the longer-term trend. Another trading expression for this is "going with the flow." From the trader's perspective, there is no other way.

For further examples of trade signals on color charts, go to trading -u.com/tradeselection.asp. To learn more about our automated indicators, which include signal arrows using multiple time frames and directional lines, go to www.trading-u.com and visit our Automated Indicators section.

Chapter 9

TRADE MANAGEMENT

Live trade management is the most important aspect of trading, and also one that is not covered in books, seminars, and webinars on trading as much as we'd like to see. It starts once you click the mouse and enter a trade. Once you put a position on, there are only three things a market can do: go up, go sideways, or go down. You are going to either make money, break even, or lose money. Most account holders will lose—not because their initial entry decision was wrong, but because they mismanaged the trade. More often than not, this means that they mistook a market that is correcting and starting to move sideways for a market that is reversing, and they exited the trade prematurely.

This is the most common mistake that retail traders make. They see a market that is consolidating under the normal flow of business, and they mistake a price shift on a lower time frame for an actual reversal and exit either with a very small profit or at a loss. Their trade entry is according to plan, but they do not have proper training and experience when it comes to differentiating between the normal ebb and flow of a market and the much more uncommon price reversal, and they end up mismanaging the trade. Given that price can do only one of three things once you are in a position (go your way, go sideways, or go against you), we are going to examine each of these occurrences and show you the proper way to manage them. But first we need to cover the subject of stops.

Stop Placement

Using stop orders to protect your account equity, like money management and wearing a seat belt in a car, is a simple, essential exercise. We identified what a stop is in *Mastering the Currency Market* (McGraw-Hill, 2009), so we can get right in to how to use them. We are going to cover three stop placement techniques: a stop placed just above (or below) the last swing high (or swing low), a stop placed just behind the extreme of a change-of-direction candle, or a stop placed just beyond significant structure such as a pivot point or trendline. Before we describe the conditions that price would need to fulfill for a stop to be filled, we need to point out that there are two kinds of stops. The first is a hard stop, where you physically place the order, and it is executed, or filled, once price trades at or beyond that price. The hard stop is generally used by swing traders and position traders, who may not be on the screen when price moves beyond the level at which they wish to exit or enter a position. The second is called a "stop-close-only," where it is up to you to monitor your trade and exit your position, or "stop" yourself out of a trade, if a candle closes at or beyond a level that triggers a signal in the opposite direction of your position.

If you are a short-term trader, also known as a day trader, and you monitor your position(s) at all times, we recommend that you use a stop-close-only. By exiting a position when price tells you to do so based on a signal going the opposite of your initial position, you will generally have smaller losses than you would if you placed a hard stop beyond a swing low or chart structure. If you are a swing trader or a position trader, you will need to place hard stops to protect your account in the event of an outsized price move or an unexpected event that increases volatility.

We definitely need to keep stop placement as automated as possible so that this decision does not distract us from the goal of identifying the most attractive setups and triggers. Many traders have an uncanny ability to place stops at a level that price finds. This is because when they are making the decision on where to place that stop, they are by default thinking about where the market would have to move in order to take their money. Most people are not thinking about making money on another successful trade when they place a hard stop. When you think about this process, it's no wonder that the market finds the majority of stop loss orders placed. It's not the broker's fault or bad luck; it is because the individual focused on where price needs to go to knock him off. And it usually does. The losing trader placed the stop at a price point that he thought was enough of a risk to take, not where it should have been placed based on the current price pattern and structure.

Markets were designed to facilitate trade. While it may seem uncanny at times, it really is commonplace for markets to move to where there are resting orders, and that means stop orders and limit orders. This is how trade is facilitated. Before we go any further, a word of caution for those of you who regularly place hard stops to exit a trade automatically if price moves a certain distance against you: if you exit a position using another type of order, such as a market order or a limit order, you must remember to cancel your resting stop order. It's too easy to forget to cancel a stop order placed from a previous trade, then open your trading account the next day and see an open position that you didn't know about because you forgot to cancel a stop and price traded to it.

Before we cover the swing stop, let's remind you what a "swing high" or "swing low" is. A swing high is the last price point at which the market recorded a bearish reversal and reversed from up to down. A "swing low" is the price point at which there was a bullish reversal from down to up. In Exhibit 9-1, we've marked the swing high and low points on a weekly gold chart. These levels are natural barriers to put your stops just beyond.

Exhibit 9-2 provides an example of a stop just beyond a swing high that would have prevented a trader from having a more serious loss.

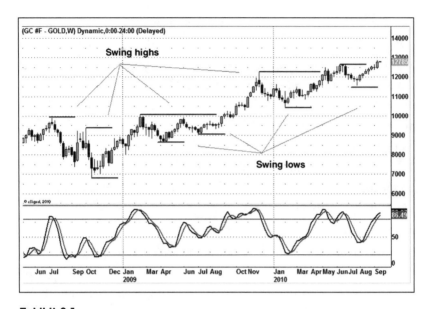

Exhibit 9-1
Source: www.esignal.com.

Exhibit 9-2
Source: www.esignal.com.

In our example, a client calls his futures broker and says: "I think silver is going to go down hard. What do you think?"

The broker says, "Well, you could be right. . . . But, silver is in a long-term bull market."

Both the client and the broker have been around the block a few times, and they both know that the broker won't talk the client out of the trade on the chance that the client is right, and because the broker would miss a commission. They both know that the observation about silver being in a bull market is a good one. After they bat the idea around for a bit, the client decides to put a smaller short position on and have the broker place a hard stop loss order above the last swing high. If he's right about silver going down, he can add to the position once he's showing a profit. If he's wrong, he'll be stopped out with a reasonable loss. Exhibit 9-2 highlights that trade.

What you need to notice in this chart is that the client was essentially taking a sell signal in the middle of a sideways trading range, which is not a good decision. Silver reacts sharply higher two days after the sell signal, and the trade is automatically exited just above that swing high, eliminating the risk of the client's balking at exiting. Once the stop is set according to your trading plan, there is no need to analyze the decision again. You can move on and look for other favorable setups, knowing that your risk on that trade has been established. A note of caution, however, on stop orders: if price moves through the stop level quickly, you need to make sure that the stop order was in fact filled, particularly if a market opens beyond your stop order on Sunday night. It is always your responsibility to monitor your account and positions.

The change-of-direction stop is placed just below the low of a bullish change-of-direction candle, or just above the high of a bearish change-of-direction candle. It can have the benefit of being lower risk, because on average it will be closer in (that is, there is less risk than with a stop placed beyond the swing point or beyond a higher-time-frame

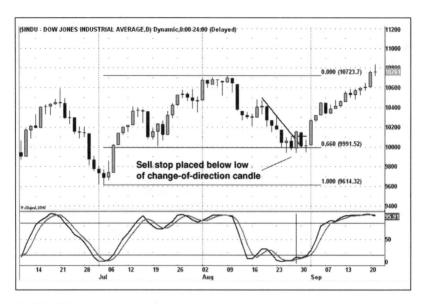

($INDU : DOW JONES INDUSTRIAL AVERAGE,D) Dynamic,0:00-24:00 (Delayed)

0.000 (10723.7)

0.660 (9991.52)

Sell stop placed below low of change-of-direction candle

1.000 (9614.32)

Exhibit 9-3
Source: www.esignal.com.

structure), but it does carry the risk of being too close to price and thus leaving the trader susceptible to getting knocked out of a trade prematurely. In Exhibit 9-3 we highlight how to use the extreme of a change-of-direction candle as a stop level.

Suppose you are a financial planner and you have a client who calls you up in late August 2010 and tells you that she wants to get back into blue chip stocks because she thinks that all the people she talks to are just too pessimistic, yet at the same time they are all sitting on a lot of cash. However, if she goes long, she doesn't want to risk staying long if stocks go into a bear market. And she doesn't want to buy options either, because you both feel that they are better sold as a hedge rather than bought as an outright position. You listen to her, and then you both agree that what she wants is to be in if stocks go up, and not be in if they go down. "It's tricky," you tell her, "but it's doable" if she is willing to take the risk of a defined loss in exchange for trying to secure the upside. You know that while the Dow Jones Industrial Average is in a downtrend currently, it has been showing indecision around the 66 percent retracement level, which also happens to be at approximately 10,000, a significant psychological level.

Two days later, the market puts in a bullish change-of-direction candle and closes above the short-term bear trendline. You get your client on the phone and tell her that you feel it's a good time to buy the ETF on the Dow Jones Industrial Average. After putting on this long position, you tell her that you plan to put on a sell stop order to protect the position just below the low of the candle that produced the buy signal. You are able to tell her exactly how much she will be risking versus how much she will make if she's right and the market rallies back to the previous high at 10,700, which would be an approximate risk/reward ratio of $100 to make $250. If price does rally back up to 10,700 in the Dow, you can then move her stop to breakeven, so that her account will enjoy the upside of any rally, while her risk is nearly eliminated by the breakeven stop. In this case the low of the change-of-direction candle ended up being the swing low, although you would not have known that at the time.

Keep in mind that you can also place a stop to initiate a trade. This might be a consideration if you are interested in putting on a position only if the market clears a particular level. You can place a stop just beyond that level, and you will automatically assume that position once price moves to the price at which you've placed the stop.

The third stop is one where we place the stop loss order beyond structure, such as a trendline or pivot point, or, more often, beyond the confluence of structure. For this example, we will use the 10-year U.S. Treasury note contract. You have taken a one-contract short position in the 10-year notes because you believe that interest rates in the United States will rise because your uncle has been telling you for years that interest rates in the United States will rise because "they just have to." But you then read in the Sunday paper that in the current economic environment, the U.S. Federal Reserve could buy 10-year Treasuries in an effort to ease interest rates if the economy were to slow. Your wife also reminds you that this same uncle who is convinced that interest rates are going higher is still a bachelor, drives a 15-year-old Chevy Cavalier, and gave you a set of baseball tickets for a wedding present.

You pull up the daily chart of the contract you are short and draw the current bear trendline, and you see that this level intersects with a monthly central pivot (see Exhibit 9-4). You realize that you definitely do not want to get caught short if the Fed starts buying Treasuries to support the economy, so you place a buy stop to buy two contracts that Sunday night just above that confluence of resistance. By buying two contracts, you will not only exit the short position, but also swing long.

A month later, with T-notes a full $4,000 higher, your wife asks you, "Hey, what ever happened to that trade Uncle Crisco talked you into?"

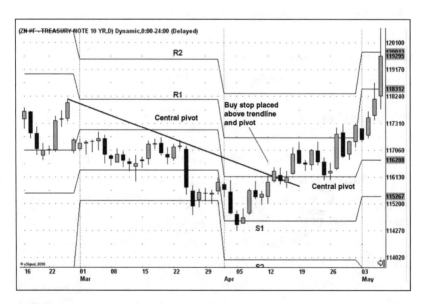

Exhibit 9-4
Source: www.esignal.com.

You say, "Baby, placing that buy stop was the best trade I ever made. And thanks for the tip on Crisco's Cavalier."

From a short-term trader's perspective, a stop is a precaution only. You will see in the next section, where we cover price failure, that more often than not, you will exit a trade when market conditions change, which will generally occur before your hard stop would get hit. The stop is in place just in case something happens in the marketplace that causes price to move quickly, and you cannot or don't react in time. By placing the stop, you have some assurance that if change comes quickly in the market, your position will be closed out for you at a specified level. This level gives you the approximate dollar amount you are risking on the trade. That dollar amount, or risk, is going to determine how many contracts you put on.

Price Follow-Through and Trade Management

Managing a trade that is exhibiting price follow-through (that is, price is going your way) is just a matter of letting the market do the work for you and not overanalyzing the position. This is easy to say, and it should be easy to do. "Let the profit run" is always great advice in trading, but doing it in practice is rarer. You will not achieve the rank of experienced trader until you can exhibit the patience and strength needed to let a profit run. Before you let a profit run, however, you need to make sure that you are in a trend trade. A trend trade is defined as a trade where either the intermediate-term or the long-term trend of the time frame you are trading is already moving in the same direction as your trade signal. An example of a trend trade would be if you were analyzing a trade where the short-term trend is setting up for a possible reversal higher, which could yield a buy signal, and the next higher time frame—the intermediate-term trend—was already higher.

The next lesson in allowing a profit to run is going to be acquiring the ability to identify sideways price movement and read the market's momentum using the MACD or some other momentum indicator. And finally, you need to know not to move your stop up or down too quickly in an attempt to "protect your profit." When you have entered a trade and it is going your way, you do not want to move your stop up too quickly until after the market has corrected back against your position and then resumed its move by posting a new high (or low) in your favor. You also want to recognize when price accelerates (that is, momentum increases), which is seen when the MACD accelerates away from its trigger line. Once that has occurred, then you may move your stop to breakeven or better.

You also will not be making a trading decision until after the candle closes or you are at least very close to the close of a candle, so if you are trading a 15-minute chart, there is no need to even follow that market that closely until just ahead of the settlement. When the candle does close, you want to check the price in relationship to its current trendline and directional line on the time frame you took the trade on to see that it is still lined up in the direction in which you took the trade. If it is, there is no decision to be made until the close of the next candle.

There are times when the price will cross a short-term trendline against your position as a market moves from trending price action to sideways or consolidating price behavior. This often happens following an impulsive move, and that frequently means that the market is not reversing, but consolidating, and the appropriate thing to do is to sit tight with the knowledge that your stop will protect your equity should price actually reverse. Under these circumstances, you may also want to use your lagging indicator, the MACD or some other oscillator that measures momentum, to keep you in a trade, particularly when price starts to consolidate or turn at a point where there is no significant support or resistance on the chart. As long as price continues to close beyond its directional line and the MACD is leading its trigger line with both moving in the same direction as your position, you can stay with the trade.

When you see price flirting with your trendline and or directional line while you are in a trade, you want to remain patient, understand that you have a stop in place to limit your loss if the market suddenly turns against you, and let the market do what it is going to do. And always follow your trading plan. One reason most people find allowing a profit to run to be so difficult to do is a combination of fear, shortsightedness, and not having a trading plan. Your trading plan should cover all potential market circumstances, which means that you should have thought these scenarios out ahead of time and written down how you will handle them. Remember, a market can only go up, go down, or go sideways. Based on the trendline and directional line, you will know what price level a market would need to close beyond for you to exit the trade. If you've done your homework and follow your plan, the market is nothing to fear. What you should fear is not following your plan!

Using Momentum Indicators

Momentum indicators, also known as center-line oscillators, are an excellent tool for keeping us in a trade when the market is moving our way, particularly if the oscillator is below the zero line and we are short, or it is above the zero line and we are long. The MACD is a lagging indicator, and one that is good at giving us a market's intermediate-term trend. Therefore, it is not going to prove valuable when markets are giving us short, quick moves, such as those we see in countertrending markets. Even a leading indicator will have trouble keeping up with a market that is moving counter to its higher-time-frame trends or that is being buffeted by conflicting economic releases or influenced by volatility in related markets. The MACD, however, being a lagging indicator and thus a trend-following indicator, can prove very useful in keeping us in extended moves, particularly when a short-term trend matures into an intermediate-term trend, or when an intermediate-term trend extends itself into a long-term trend. It can be particularly

valuable when it is telling us to stay in a position despite the fact that
a leading indicator is telling us to exit.

Relying on a lagging indicator to keep you in a trade can increase
your risk also, which means that you need to always utilize a stop order
to protect your account balance. The simplest function of the MACD
is that it produces a buy signal when the MACD line crosses above its
trigger line, and it produces a sell signal when the MACD crosses
below its trigger line. This can be very effective in helping you to manage a trade, and specifically to let a profit run when you see price direction on the lower time frames line up with direction on the higher
time frames, despite what leading indicators, and even price itself, are
showing you on the lower time frames.

On the EUR-USD 240-minute chart in Exhibit 9-5 in August of 2010,
we've circled those periods where the market consolidated after a down
move and gave us a change of direction on the first correction and a

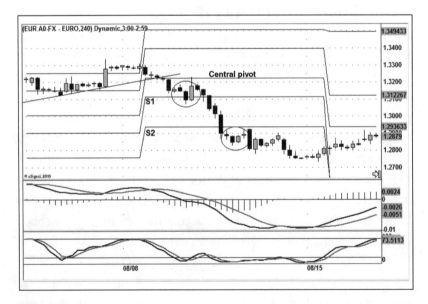

Exhibit 9-5
Source: www.esignal.com.

trendline breach on a closing basis on the second correction. Those indications could not, however, overcome resistance levels in the form of the pivots, nor did they shift the MACD's trigger lines. This is a great example of using a lagging indicator (the MACD) properly to keep you in what turned out to be a trend trade. What was important to recognize in both cases was that price closed below support prior to correcting. Had the support held and had price then closed above the pivots after testing them, it would have been unlikely that we would have stayed in the trade the whole way down. It was the close below support that encouraged us to use the lagging indicator to stay with the trade.

Exhibit 9-6 shows the same market and the same chart, minus the pivot points, but with the previous daily directional lines in place, so you can see how, despite short-term indications to exit, such as 240-minute changes of directions and stochastic crosses, by following the MACD and by maintaining higher-time-frame confirmation, we were able to maximize the profit on the trade.

Exhibit 9-6
Source: www.esignal.com.

When you are making the decision to use the MACD to keep you in a trade, despite a change of direction and a trendline break and stochastic cross against you, keep in mind that you are essentially making a determination that price is just pausing, or consolidating, before a resumption of the previous move, and you want to make sure that the price turn against you is not occurring on significant support or resistance (such as a trendline, a pivot point, or a previous weekly or monthly high or low), and that the higher-time-frame trend is still in your favor.

In the example in Exhibits 9-5 and 9-6, it's also very important that the MACD crossed below zero earlier in the move, indicating an intermediate-term trend shift. You would generally not use the MACD to keep you in a trade that long unless you had a MACD zero line cross in your favor. And a good rule of thumb is to use the MACD to keep you in a trade only when a price move is maintaining higher-time-frame confirmation. Exhibit 9-7 is an example of a weekly chart where the MACD proved an excellent indicator for keeping us in an extended up move.

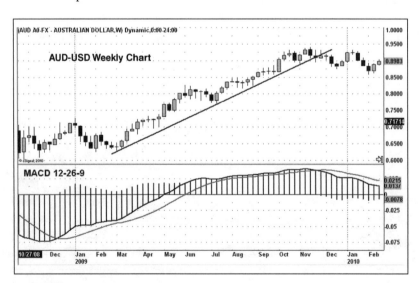

Exhibit 9-7
Source: www.esignal.com.

Trading Multiple Contracts

Just as you are going to be making decisions using a higher-time-frame chart to identify setups, you are going to have a choice as to which time frame to use to manage a trade on once you are in it. This is where trading multiple contracts is going to help you. In Forex, we have the choice of trading in a multiple as low as $1,000 per contract, which is called a "micro." If you buy or sell a $10,000 block of currency, also known as a "mini," you always have the choice of taking a portion of that position off. This can be a convenience.

A rule of thumb is that if you are in a position (a trade) and it is going your way, but price starts to show indecision on a lower time frame in the form of individual candle behavior, on a significant support or resistance level, such as a pivot point, or on a previous daily or weekly high or low, and we start to see similar candle behavior on the higher time frame (what we call "like behavior"), we can lock in a profit by taking one-half to two-thirds of the position off, and then placing a breakeven stop on the balance of the position. Once you've trimmed your position in this manner and significantly reduced the likelihood of a loss, you will be in a much better mental state to manage the balance of your position with an eye on letting a profit run.

Exhibit 9-8 is an example of "like behavior" that is constantly playing out in the currency markets on all time frames. Price gives us a change of direction on the 240-minute chart in the top panel (circled) and closes above the weekly S1. On the higher-time-frame daily chart, we see price probe below the long-term trendline but then close above it. This combination of activity is enough to get us to cover two-thirds of our short position based on the price action on the 240-minute chart. We then see price climb above the weekly central pivot on the 240-minute chart, followed by a change-of-direction candle on the daily chart (circled).

We can take the change-of-direction candle on the daily chart as a signal to exit any remaining short position, or at least place a buy stop

Exhibit 9-8
Source: www.esignal.com.

above the daily central pivot. By managing the trade this way, we both protected our profits and left ourselves in a position to let a profit run should the lower-time-frame signal prove to be just a price pause and not a price reversal. What's important to recognize is that there was a change of direction on support on the lower-time-frame 240-minute chart, followed the next day by a change-of-direction candle on support on the higher-time-frame daily chart.

In the example in Exhibit 9-9, price shows two shooting stars below R2 along with negative divergence on the MACD. This tells us that higher prices are being rejected, and the MACD is telling us that price

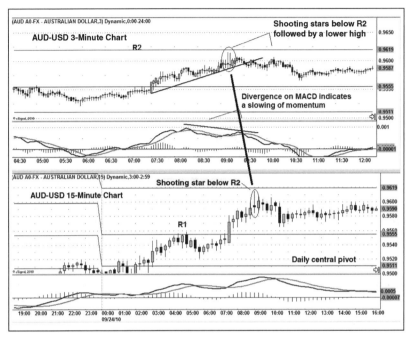

Exhibit 9-9
Source: www.esignal.com.

momentum is decreasing. Minutes later, we get a shooting star on the 15-minute chart. This is an indication that we should consider exiting a portion of our position on a signal on the lower-time-frame 3-minute chart to protect a profit rather than wait for a signal on the higher-time-frame 15-minute chart. This proves a more profitable way to manage the trade, as price slumps an hour and a half later and then goes flat for the rest of the session. This indecisive price action on the lower time frame creates "like behavior" on the higher-time-frame chart.

What like behavior reminds us of is that market price action typifies fractal geometry, where what happens on the higher time frames is replicated on the lower time frames. Because of this, we can have confidence that before a market turns around on a higher time frame, such as a weekly or a monthly chart, it will exhibit indecision followed by a change of direction on the lower time frames first. Because of this, we can be also assured that what is occurring on one chart is being replicated on the next lower time frame. This is very helpful in guiding us to exit positions in a timely manner and in protecting our trading capital. It is subtle hints such as these that you will need to see in making the all-important decision as to whether to allow a profit to run because of the price action and momentum on the higher time frame, or to heed the price action relative to structure and momentum on the lower time frame by taking one-half to two-thirds of the position off and managing the balance of the position on the higher time frame, on the chance that the price move extends itself.

There is a lot to be said for monitoring higher-time-frame structure, such as monthly and weekly pivots and retracements, and being quick to take a portion of your position off at these levels following signs of indecision on the lower time frames.

Exhibit 9-10 shows a daily chart of EUR-JPY for the second half of 2009, and we can see how well served we would have been by exiting a portion of our position on the first test of a monthly pivot point after a sustained move, and on indecisive price action on the lower time frames, where price couldn't hold beyond the structure, rather than waiting for a change of direction and a trendline break and stochastic cross first on the daily chart. Keep in mind that we need to exit only a portion of our position in case the market continues to move in our direction. Also keep in mind that because market behavior typifies fractal geometry, we are going to see like behavior between time frames spaced four to six times apart, meaning that we will see indecision and change of direction on the lower time frames first. A serious determinant of your success as a trader will be your ability to stay patient and let the market work for you. What is going to help you do this is trading multiple contracts and learning how to exit a portion of your position against existing support or resistance and managing the

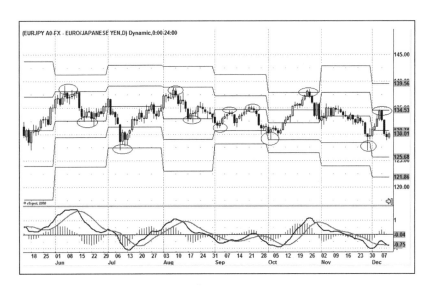

Exhibit 9-10
Source: www.esignal.com.

balance of the position on the higher time frame, using change of direction, trendline breaks, and the stochastic cross.

We talk a lot about the higher-time-frame trends because it is the direction of those trends that differentiates between trend trades and countertrend trades. It is always sound advice to remind even experienced traders to stick with trend trades. Despite that, there will come times where you will probably find a countertrend setup and signal on historical structure, with divergence, and with a favorable risk/reward ratio that is hard to pass up. Under circumstances such as these, you need to know that however attractive the setup may be, it is a countertrend signal, and you will need to manage it differently.

For countertrend signals, we do not use a momentum indicator to manage the trade; we would exit the trade on the first trendline and directional-line breach on a closing basis against our position. On the other hand, if the trade goes our way and a short-term trend

Exhibit 9-11
Source: www.esignal.com.

shift leads to an intermediate-term trend shift, meaning that the trade shifted to a trend trade, then you can bring in the momentum indicator to help keep you in the trade. Exhibit 9-11 is an example of a trade that started out countertrend and extended into a trend move. By initially managing the trade using a trendline and directional line, you remain long until price clears an intermediate-term bear trendline and a MACD zero-line cross, which confirms an intermediate-term trend shift. At this point, you can manage the trade using the MACD.

Sideways Price Action and Trade Management

Markets historically move sideways more than they trend. Sideways price channels, or "rectangles," as we described them in *Mastering the Currency Market*, are common price formations that we come across in our day-to-day trading and analysis. They can also pose pitfalls for trend traders who don't fully understand higher-time-frame confirmation or who don't use directional lines. It is imperative that we understand how sideways ranges occur and how they play out. The first thing we need to understand is that these are time periods during which the market is taking a breather, or consolidating after an impulsive price move. They are generally created following an extended directional price move, but they can occur over the course of slower directional moves also. It's important to remember that we will see many more sideways ranges than market tops or bottoms in our trading careers. Exhibit 9-12 is an example of price going sideways and the technical indicators telling us it may be reversing.

Let's analyze the sideways price formation created in the GBP-USD in the first half of 2008 in Exhibit 9-12 so that we can start to understand how they form, which will help us to recognize them as they are occurring. The first indication that a sideways range is in the making is a change-of-direction candle. This tells us that the current trend is

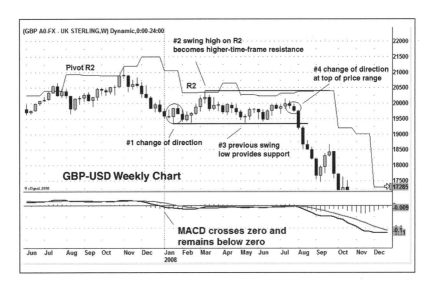

Exhibit 9-12
Source: www.esignal.com.

pausing, and while it is one of the signals that can indicate that a shift in the short-term trend is occurring, it is more likely to signal the beginning of a sideways range than to signal an actual trend reversal. We can say this with confidence because of the trending nature of markets. They will consolidate more times than they reverse.

The second indicator that a sideways range is being built is price failing to hold above higher-time-frame resistance in the form of monthly R2; there was also the confluence of a 50 percent retracement level (not marked) in this same area. The third indicator was price holding above the pre-change-of-direction swing low, followed by a retest of the higher-time-frame resistance just before number 4, a bearish change-of-direction candle and a sharp sell-off to break out of the price range. Change-of-direction candles at the extremes of large price ranges often provide attractive setups and signals.

In the example of a sideways price range in AUD-JPY in Exhibit 9-13, we see a similar sequence of events play out, starting with the change of direction on both the daily and weekly charts, only this time price finds higher-time-frame support at the confluence of its monthly central pivot point and the 50 percent retracement level of the previous month's rally. Then we again see the familiar pattern of the swing high created after that first price bounce proving resistance, and the market ranging sideways between that first swing low and swing high—which later provide the structure for future weekly and monthly directional lines—until it breaks above resistance early in October 2009.

Notice how after support held twice in September, the MACD, while having crossed its trigger line twice, just meandered sideways, helping us to identify a directionless market. A sideways MACD also tells us that the market has no momentum, so we will need to be extra patient in waiting for a tradable move, and know that price will have to close above or below the sideways range before we can take a trade. Regardless of favorable price pattern and favorable

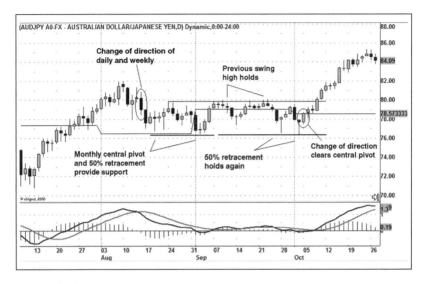

Exhibit 9-13
Source: www.esignal.com.

structure, if a market is showing low momentum, it isn't going to be worth trading.

By now you should be seeing a pattern here. Just like any trend, a sideways pattern is going to begin with a change of direction and end with a change of direction. Swing highs and lows, which most often occur on monthly pivots, retracements, or trendlines, become future directional lines as price moves forward through time. We chose the previous examples of higher-time-frame sideways formations because they are easier to analyze than the lower-time-frame price ranges and consolidation periods, which can prove trickier to trade though. It is those times when a trader takes a trade on the 240- or 60-minute time frames and the market gives sideways price action on the lower time frames that can be hardest to sit through without exiting early and missing further opportunity. Exhibit 9-14 provides a good example of this.

We get a buy signal on this 60-minute AUD-USD chart following a double bottom on pivot resistance 1 with the trends on the daily and

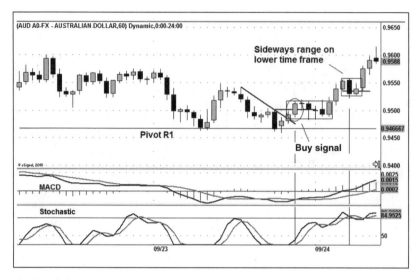

Exhibit 9-14
Source: www.esignal.com.

weekly charts already higher. After weathering initial sideways price action, price does accelerate higher, turning the 240-minute trend higher. But then price gives a change-of-direction candle on the 60-minute chart followed by a stochastic bear cross. The proper way to manage this trade would be to stay patient because we know that the 240-minute chart is still higher, and to monitor the momentum via the MACD because we know that we are in a trend trade. The MACD is holding steady, so we can see that the momentum is still positive, telling us that the change-of-direction candle is probably not a reversal.

If you are especially nervous regarding a loss, you can place a breakeven stop on the trade, but then you risk getting stopped out prematurely at the low of the correction. Remember, markets correct and consolidate more than they actually reverse, so you know that more often than not, a change-of-direction candle is signifying a pause or correction. If you can weather the correction, you are on your way to learning the most important aspect of trading, which is letting a profit run. In the trade example in Exhibit 9-14, the market does resume its uptrend and post a higher high, despite that change-of-direction candle and stochastic cross. The key here is to be patient and to use the lagging indicator (MACD) because the trends were up on the higher time frames.

Let's analyze one more sideways formation, again on an intraday chart (see Exhibit 9-15). This time we do not get a change of direction, but we do get successive closes below the central pivot, and a stochastic bear cross.

We should keep calm and determined to maintain our long position because of the large benchmark candle, which closed above the central pivot and which created our directional line, and the MACD. The MACD flattening out should tip us off that while momentum is slowing, it is still above zero, and that price has just gone into a rectangle as it consolidates its earlier gains.

Exhibit 9-15
Source: www.esignal.com.

If you are to be successful as a trend trader, you are going to have to learn to be patient and stay with your position when momentum slows and the market you are in goes sideways. This is going to happen to you far more often than those times where price follows through for you during the majority of the trading session. The key is in recognizing that despite the trendline break and the directional-line shift, momentum is still holding. You can take off a portion of your position based on that short-term trend shift, but maintain the balance of the position as long as momentum is telling you to do so. If you get nervous at the prospect of maintaining a position against that short-term trend shift, then by all means place a breakeven stop on the original position.

Price Failure and Trade Management

When a trade we have entered does not follow through, what happens is that we get a setup and signal in the opposite direction, and if it has enough momentum, this reverses the previous trend. This can happen on the very candle that we took as a signal, and it can happen whether you are in a trend trade or a countertrend trade. This is why it is imperative that you do not get attached to a position and that you understand that a setup can develop at any time and a trade signal can follow. You will be far better off paying attention to developing setups and trade signals rather than reading or hearing about the markets on blogs and cable news shows, or worse, paying attention only to those items that seem to substantiate your existing opinion and position.

We generally enter trades using a change of direction in price and/or leading technical indicators before a lagging indicator such as the MACD can cross. Therefore, an excellent hint that price may be failing after we take a signal is that the MACD never crosses in our favor. When this occurs, it is telling us that there is not yet momentum behind the signal that we took. We need to find a balance between being patient and allowing the trade to develop in our favor, and being alert to exit the trade on either a close above the high of the candle we entered on or a change of direction and stochastic cross. We may have placed a stop loss order against our position also, in which case we need to remember to cancel that order once we exit the trade based on a new signal against our position.

As you go on to back-test and demo trade the tactics we've taught you, you will find that you will be exiting trades before your stops are filled far more times than you will actually be taken out of a trade by a stop. Again, it's important that you remember to check your orders to make sure you did not leave any working stop or limit orders on your platform once you've exited a trade.

In the example in Exhibit 9-16, we take a sell signal in line with the overall trend, as identified by the bear trendline and pivot points, and place a buy stop order just above the last swing high. When we took the trade, however, the MACD line was slightly above its trigger line,

Exhibit 9-16
Source: www.esignal.com.

indicating low momentum in the market at that time. Under these circumstances, we need to stay patient and watch what the market does next, knowing that our risk is limited by the buy stop. Price does give us a new low, but the MACD never does cross below its trigger line. And the lower low is followed by a bullish change-of-direction candle that closes above the pivot and the bear trendline and is accompanied by a stochastic bull cross. This is a buy signal, and because the MACD is above its trigger line, we have no choice but to exit the short position with a loss.

You also need to be reminded that you are going to manage a trade differently depending on whether it is a trend trade or a countertrend trade. A countertrend trade is defined as a trade where trend in the next higher time trend is opposite to the signal. For example, the signal you are analyzing indicates that the short-term trend may be shifting higher, yet the intermediate-term trend is still lower. No matter how attractive a countertrend trade looks when you are entering it, you have to exit it on the first signal that goes against your position, regardless of momentum. From a trade management perspective, the difference between a countertrend trade and a trend trade is that we do not use a momentum indicator for trade management in a countertrend trade until the next higher-time-frame trend that was counter to the position at the time of entry reverses. Exhibit 9-17 highlights why we need to exit a countertrend trade on the first signal. Had the trader not been conscious of being in a countertrend trade and had tried to manage the trade using a momentum indicator, she would have, in trader jargon, "gotten her lungs ripped out" as the intermediate-term trend, which remained in line with the long-term trend, reasserted itself.

It's important that the trader knows ahead the difference between managing trend trades and managing countertrend trades. In Exhibit 9-18, we've highlighted the differences for you.

For further examples of these trade management techniques on color charts, go to trading-u.com/tradeselection and use the password tradingu.

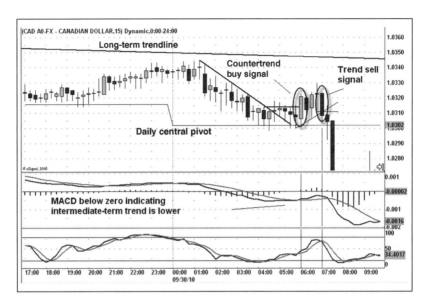

Exhibit 9-17
Source: www.esignal.com.

Trade Management for Trend versus Countertrend	Trend Trigger	Countertrend Trigger
Entry and management	Trendline and directional-line break on closing basis with stochastic confirmation; manage using MACD	Trendline and directional-line break on closing basis with stochastic confirmation; manage using stochastic cross
Exit	Exit 1/2 to 2/3 of position on trendline and directional-line break on closing basis against structure; exit balance on MACD cross	Trendline and directional-line break on closing basis with stochastic confirmation

Exhibit 9-18
Source: www.esignal.com.

Live trade management is the most important aspect of trading, and it will determine whether or not you are a successful trader. As with any professional endeavor, you need a straightforward plan to follow before you find yourself in a live trade, and you need experience in executing that plan. This book goes a long way in providing the information you will need to construct that plan, but it will be up to you to put in the time trading live markets in a demo account to get that experience.

If you already have a trading plan and are experienced, and you are considering adding new wrinkles that you learned from this book or in our courses, you need to rewrite your plan to include the new inputs. And you need to go back to a demo account or micro account and get used to trading your new plan in live markets prior to risking your money. Don't fall into the trap of thinking that a demo account or micro contracts don't give you "real" experience. You will know what is at stake for your future, and we believe that if you follow your trading plan and get the desired results over a period measured in many months, regardless of the contract size, you will be able to continue that success going forward.

Chapter 10

TRADE EXAMPLES
WITH TRADING PLANS

B efore we highlight trade examples, let's identify the three different kinds of trades we are going to cover. The first is a trend trade,
also called a position trade, which is taken on a daily chart and is
in line with the trend on the weekly and/or monthly chart. The second
is a swing trade, which is one taken on a chart of any time frame
following a signal on just that time frame, regardless of the higher-
time-frame trends. And the third is a day trade, which can be either
a trend trade or a countertrend trade, but which is not carried into
the next session. The common thread in all these trades is that prior
to entering them, you need to see short-term momentum in your
favor and structure that is supportive of the trade signal. When you
see those two technical conditions in place, you can have some assurance that the current risk environment (fundamentals) is favorable
for that trade or investment.

Trend Trading

The trend trade on the daily chart is taken only based on a signal on that
chart and can be managed and exited only based on a signal on the daily
chart. It is the most desirable for professional traders because it offers the
most favorable risk/reward scenario. Because it is being managed on the

daily time frame and the entry is in line with the weekly and/or monthly trend, it puts the trader in a position to maximize her gains. The risk on the trade, however, is also higher because daily moves are bigger than intraday moves, so it's important that the trader or investor go with an appropriate position size for her bank account and temperament.

There are many traders or investors who got in at the right time in the right market, but who exited prematurely because they weren't mentally equipped to exhibit patience and discipline in the face of a fluctuating account balance. And that doesn't mean just when the trade is going against them. Often a trade will go your way, and you'll start comparing that small profit to a material possession. Before you know it, you've talked yourself into taking the profit with a plan to get a new coat and get back in the trade again at a more advantageous price. You end up booking a small profit, but the train just keeps on rolling without you, and you miss out on the larger opportunity. To help ensure that you don't make a mistake in the management of the trade, we have provided a trading plan for you.

Trend Trading Plan

Method. Trend trading on the daily chart.

Setup. Trendline and directional-line penetration on the daily chart, in the same direction as the short-term trend on the weekly chart.

Trigger. Price closes beyond both a trendline and the daily and weekly directional lines.

Management. Place a GTC (good till canceled) stop loss order beyond the last swing high (or low). If price goes against the trade initially, but the trade is not stopped out, and the MACD remains crossed in favor of the trade, stay with the position. If the MACD was never crossed in favor of the trade, exit on the first close below the low of the signal candle (the signal candle is the candle that first gave the signal), and remember to cancel

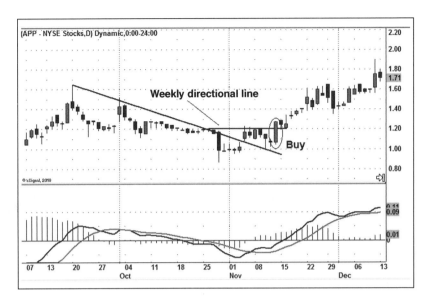

Exhibit 10-1
Source: www.esignal.com.

your stop order. If the trade goes in your favor, do not exit until the MACD crosses against your position. Once you do exit, remember to cancel your stop order.

The chart in Exhibit 10-1 is an example of a trend trade in Apple stock on the daily chart, using this trading plan. By using this plan, you would have been able to catch a nice rally (as of this writing, you would still be in the trade), and you could take comfort in knowing that you are following a trading plan that is not going to change.

In Exhibit 10-2, we've provided an example of another trade using the same trading plan, this time in the corn futures market. After the market initially sold off following the sell signal, it recovered and started to move back higher, and the trader would have had to exit the trade once the MACD crossed back up, against the trade. Keep in mind that before you take a trade like this, you have to be willing to

Exhibit 10-2
Source: www.esignal.com.

risk the trade to beyond that swing high in early November, which would have been a larger risk than the reward turned out to be.

Exhibit 10-3 provides an example of a trade in the EUR-USD market using this same trading plan. The thing you should always remember about trading is that it looks very simple on a black-and-white chart in a book, and it can be. Depending on your own experience and thought process, however, it can become anything but simple. The way to prevent your own mind from thinking back and comparing the current situation to a past situation or from casting forward and imagining an outcome is to have a trading plan and believe in that plan, so that you follow it without hesitation.

Swing Trading

Swing trading is a form of trading in which you are taking each signal that comes up, regardless of direction. The swing trader has

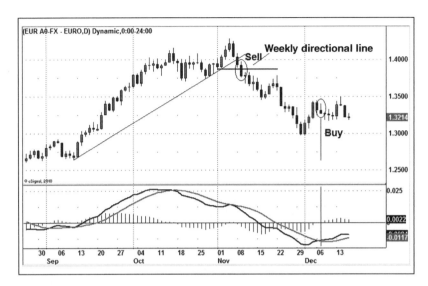

Exhibit 10-3
Source: www.esignal.com.

no market opinion and executes trade signals as they occur. The
strategy behind swing trading is that by taking every trade signal,
the trader will catch the larger trend trades and legitimate reversals
by default.

In Chapter 3, we touched on countertrending markets and how we
can recognize them ahead of time using our directional lines. If price
is below the weekly directional line but above the daily directional
line, then we know that this market is in a countertrending environment. Countertrending markets, those without a noticeable directional bias, are ideal markets to swing trade in. Here is a swing trading
plan to follow to help us stay on point.

Swing Trading Plan

Method. Swing trading on a 240- or 60-minute chart.

Setup. Trendline bordering a directional move when price is between
its higher-time-frame directional lines. (Higher-time-frame

directional lines are monthly and weekly, weekly and daily, or daily and 240-minute.)

Trigger. A price close beyond a trendline.

Management. Place a GTC (good till canceled) stop loss order beyond the last swing high (or low). Update the new trendline, and exit the trade at the directional line or when the new trendline is penetrated on a closing basis.

In Exhibit 10-4, we see the EUR-USD 60-minute chart, where price is pinned between the weekly directional line above and the daily directional line below and just zigzags back and forth. Despite there being no real directional bias, the market does respect its short-term trendlines, making a breach of the trendline on a closing basis a simple yet effective trade trigger, with the exit on the trade coming when it touches one of the directional lines or when a trendline gives way.

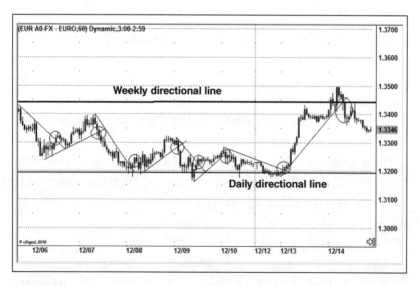

Exhibit 10-4

Source: www.esignal.com.

Exhibit 10-5
Source: www.esignal.com.

The next example is the S&P 500 stock index future in Exhibit 10-5, where we see price in a countertrending pattern below the weekly directional line and above the daily directional line. Price retests the daily line, then changes direction higher and closes above the bear trendline to give us a swing trade buy signal.

Anytime the higher-time-frame trends are counter to each other, we define this as a countertrending environment. We have not spent a lot of time on countertrending tactics in this book because countertrending markets tend to be choppier and trickier to trade than trending markets. It's far better to be patient and wait for trending markets, but we understand that traders don't always have that luxury. Your best defense as a trend trader will be knowing how to countertrend trade, and before you can do that, you need to be able to recognize when you are in a countertrending environment. The countertrend environment is also conducive for swing trading, where a directional

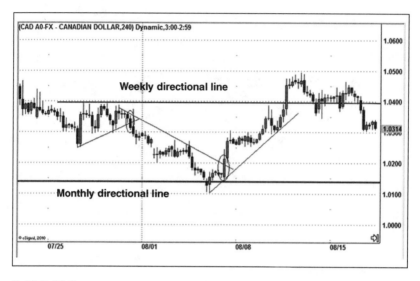

Exhibit 10-6
Source: www.esignal.com.

bias or market thesis is not needed, as you are just taking the signals as they come up. On an intraday chart such as a 60- or 240-minute chart, swing trades can provide opportunities if you know what you're doing.

In the USD-CAD chart in Exhibit 10-6, we see how this market shifted into a countertrending environment in August of 2010, which eventually gave swing traders a good buy signal following the breach of a trendline after price bounced off the monthly directional line.

As we said before, countertrending environments have their challenges. Mainly, you need to make decisions more quickly. These environments can be especially challenging for market participants who put weight on the "why" of price movement because in these environments, there is no "why" other than that price closed above or below an arbitrary line. This is one reason why floor traders were able to flourish in the twentieth century; they never concerned themselves with the "why" of price action. There was very little thoughtfulness behind making money in a trading pit. You bought downticks and you sold upticks because you knew that more than 70 percent of the time, there was little risk (no market-moving influences), so markets moved sideways. On the stock side of the business, you knew that people put a percentage of their earnings into their 401(k)s or investment programs every payday, so you had a good idea that twice a month you would get an influx of real money into blue chip stocks and other asset-class markets. If there was a time to step out and make a directional play, it was when there was no obvious risk (negative fundamentals) in the news, and the tax-free 401(k) money was flowing in at the beginning and middle of the month.

All things being equal, workers' savings and investments going into asset-class markets ensured a regular bid, while markets tended toward sideways movement in between. If there was risk (economic contraction), that risk would offset the investment flows until it worked its way through the system and the regular investment flows timed to workers' pay schedules eventually offset the funds exiting the market out of fear. The net effect of conflicting influences is often choppy, directionless trading, which we identify using our directional lines. For most investors and traders, countertrend markets should be avoided until trending markets resume. Exhibit 10-6 highlights this dynamic.

The market in Exhibit 10-7 is a daily chart of the stock of GE. We can see that in mid-October, risk comes into the market, and the stock drops sharply. The stock is still above its weekly directional line, but below its monthly directional line. We now know that it is in a countertrend environment, meaning that choppy, directionless trade could ensue—which it does. We make the decision not to trade in this environment. Price tries to mount a rally in early November, but slumps in mid-November, which tells us that the risk in the market is offsetting the 401(k) inflows. In late November, price is between the weekly and daily directional lines after finding support at approximately 15.50, so we are again in a countertrending environment.

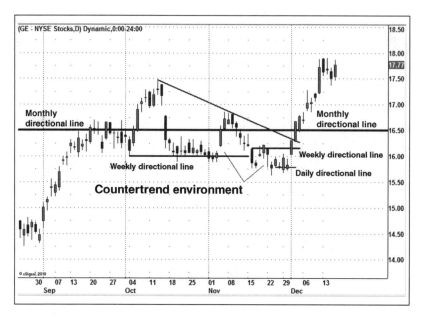

Exhibit 10-7
Source: www.esignal.com.

But look what happens very quickly at the beginning of December. Inflows into the stock propel it higher; the trends on the weekly and daily charts align themselves on December 1; GE clears the monthly directional line on December 2, leaving the monthly, weekly, and daily trends all pointed higher; and we see a sharp rally. It's invaluable to know when the trends are aligned, but you won't be able to define that without knowing how to measure when they are counter to each other.

While countertrending markets often lend themselves to swing trading, you can swing trade in any market at any time. Perhaps you notice that crude oil futures have just completed a 50 percent retracement (see Exhibit 10-8). You then see price give a bullish change of direction following a trendline penetration on a closing basis, and you know that this is a trade trigger, so you take the swing trade. You aren't sure

Exhibit 10-8
Source: www.esignal.com.

of the long-term or intermediate-term trend, but you know that this is a buy trigger on the daily chart.

You can swing trade on any time frame, and most professional traders do. In the chart in Exhibit 10-9, crude oil futures bottom out just above pivot support 2, then give a buy signal above both a bear trendline and pivot support 1. Regardless of what the overall trends were before, this swing trade was a success. The strategy behind swing trading, once again, is that by taking every signal, you will by default catch the bigger trend trades.

Day Trading

From a trading perspective, the only real difference between day trading and position trading or swing trading is that you have to allow for the risk brought on by the various economic releases occurring over

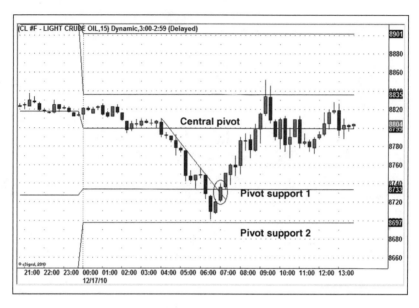

Exhibit 10-9
Source: www.esignal.com.

a shorter time period. In day trading, you are using shorter-term charts and shorter-term structure; however, you will be using them the same way as you would on the higher time frames. The reason such a high percentage of people fail when it comes to day trading is that as a day trader, you need to make more decisions per day, and you have to make those decisions more quickly, which increases the likelihood of a mistake. Throw in trading around or through economic releases, and day trading becomes all the more complex.

The way to put the odds in your favor as a day trader is going to be to trade with the higher-time-frame trends and exit positions just ahead of major economic releases. Regardless of how low a time frame you are trading, you will have an easier time of it if you are patient enough to wait for setups and trade triggers in the same direction as the weekly, daily, and four-hour trends, and avoid the added risk of holding trades through major economic releases. For day trading, we will use the

Exhibit 10-10
Source: www.esignal.com.

trading plans we have given for trend trading and swing trading and just replace those higher-time-frame charts with lower-time-frame charts such as the 60-minute, 15-minute, or even 5-minute. Exhibit 10-10 highlights a day trade in the British pound. Not only were those higher time frames aligned, but on this Friday there happened to be no economic releases.

What was interesting for us about this particular setup and signal was that the day before, you had an identical trade (see where the bull trendline started) that stopped short of accelerating lower; the market then recovered and traded higher and sideways for another 18 hours before giving another sell signal, which proved to be much larger and deeper. On both occasions, the higher time frames were aligned, but on Friday, December 17, there were no economic releases scheduled, so that when price did roll lower again, there was less risk in being short. All the news (speed bumps, in the eyes of day traders) was out of the way, increasing the likelihood that price would continue going down the path it was already on.

The way to day trade around economic releases is to exit trades inside of 15 minutes of the number and observe price immediately following the release to see if it holds its previous trend. If the 3-minute chart closes in line with the 15-minute chart following the news, then you can reenter the market in the same direction it was moving before the number. If the economic release reverses the market, then you want to be patient and wait to see whether that market is reversing on the higher time frames as well.

Many traders don't understand the influence of the higher-time-frame trends, and the weekly trend in particular, on intraday price action. Even experienced traders have questioned us as to how the trend on the weekly chart can affect direction intraday, yet we know from experience that you will always be better served by keeping yourself positioned in the direction of those higher-time-frame charts. In Exhibit 10-11, we've marked all the previous weekly directional lines on this weekly chart of the EUR-USD, and we've circled those few times that price recorded a weekly shift for the 18 months between January 2009 and June 2010.

When you look at Exhibit 10-11 and you understand the concept of a directional line (the low of the highest closing candle in an uptrend, or the high of the lowest closing candle in an downtrend) to identify trend and direction, you start to ask yourself why, even as a day trader, would you go against the weekly trend? Only three times over an 18-month period—early March 2009, late October 2009, and June 2010, all circled—did we see weekly shifts, and all three times they proved to be major trend changes! Now think to yourself, how would you have performed if you had traded only with the weekly trend on an intraday basis?

Exhibit 10-12 is another example of how the directional lines help us to identify the different trends at play in a market that help us with

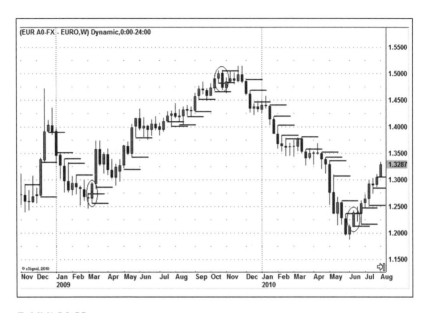

Exhibit 10-11

Source: www.esignal.com.

Exhibit 10-12

Source: www.esignal.com.

our day trade selection. The weekly trend (not pictured) is already down, as is the daily trend. The 60-minute trend is lower, while the 240-minute trend is in the process of shifting lower. With all time frames down like this going into the U.S. session, EUR-USD just can't recover, and once it closes below a trendline at approximately 8:15 a.m., the price accelerates lower.

Directional lines are helpful to us for trade selection because they provide definition, on which we can base rules for identifying trending and countertrending markets; there are, however, other effective means for identifying day trade setups and signals. In Chapter 3 and Chapter 7, we touched on channel lines, which are also helpful in identifying both trend and countertrend setups. We can use the same swing trading plan, just substituting channel lines for directional lines. In Exhibit 10-13, we've placed channel lines on this AUD-USD intraday chart and marked a countertrend sell

Exhibit 10-13
Source: www.esignal.com.

Exhibit 10-14
Source: www.esignal.com.

signal on December 15 against the top of the channel, which also showed negative divergence.

Exhibit 10-14 provides another good example of channel lines helping us to define a market's pattern and to identify on December 15, on the right side of the chart, when that market was rolling over from countertrending behavior to trending behavior.

At its technical base, trading comes down to one of two root methods: either you are trading with the trend, or you are trading counter to it. Given that every trend starts out as a countertrend at some point, and that you can't make money unless you are in the market, there is sound logic for experienced traders to swing trade. For most speculative account holders, however, who trade out of curiosity, or as a hobby, or in hopes of making it a second career, trend trading is the way to go because it helps keep them out of trouble, allows them more time to make a trading decision, and has a more favorable risk/ reward ratio.

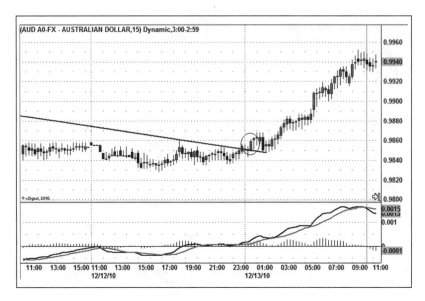

Exhibit 10-15
Source: www.esignal.com.

One of the great paradoxes of trading is how we can take something that is essentially as simple as buying low and selling high and put our own complicated stamp on it. Exhibit 10-15 is a great example of how simple trading can be if you follow a plan and don't consider your previous trading experiences or your future expectations relevant.

The Australian dollar in December of 2010 is a market that is in an uptrend on its monthly trend and is showing a bullish price pattern on both its weekly and its daily charts. This trade on the 15-minute chart is just a matter of buying a bear trendline break and holding the trade until the momentum indicator crosses down. It's a very simple and straightforward technique (the trading plan is spelled out earlier in this chapter in the section on trend trading; just substitute intraday chart for daily chart), yet the majority of students will consistently find a way to fail to capitalize on it as they should. Trading will always be more than 90 percent psychological for most of us, because money, which is why we trade, can complicate the human thought process as much as, if not more than, even love. As a trader, you must remind yourself that the only thing you must focus on is following your trading plan without error, which means taking only actions that are spelled out for you ahead of time. There is no doubt about it: there are different ways to approach trading successfully, and the one common theme that they all have is having a trading plan and following it.

CONCLUSION

Realistic Expectations

Buying and selling a market in the expectation of a higher rate of return than is currently available to you, be it in a demo account or with your hard-earned money in a live account, should be seen as just the tip of a very large iceberg. You will need to take the information provided in the pages of this book and boil it down to a one- or two-page trading plan. When you are ready to write out your own trading plan go to the table of contents of this book and write down the chapter titles for Chapters 3, 7, 8 and 9.

- Market Overview
- Trade Setup
- Trigger Defined and Trade Entered
- Trade Management

These will be the headers for the most important parts of your plan. Being able to produce consistent results with that plan will take consistent effort on your part, though. Success in any endeavor, particularly one that is as challenging as following a trading plan in live markets, is just a matter of taking the initiative to study the educational material extensively and then being at the right place at the right time to execute what you've been taught. A lot of professionals will tell you that to achieve success, you need to have a goal. In trading, that goal should be to not make errors (take any action outside of your trading plan) and to show up at your workstation early every day. You will find that being early is going to help you be better prepared, and over the course of months and years, it will help you to find more winning trades.

It's also very important that you have realistic expectations concerning both how long it will take you to learn to trade and how much of a rate of return you can expect from trading. We have a client, Samuel, who is an eye surgeon who has adopted a very patient attitude in learning to trade. He realizes that after many years of schooling, the first time he suited up to enter the operating room, he was not nearly as confident or as skilled a surgeon as he is today. He realizes that when it comes to trading, the process of acquiring experience isn't any different, and he doesn't have to make that many trades in order to be successful. He also has the added comfort of knowing that he can be patient in waiting for a setup and signal that he's comfortable with. He is, in two words, "reality oriented." Given that he can trade only on his days off, he often uses a demo account so that he can get in as many trades as possible and get the experience of managing them in a live market according to his plan. If he sees a setup and signal that isn't optimal based on his experience in gauging structure and momentum, he will still take the trade, but in the demo account. If he sees a trade setup and signal that fits all of the criteria in his plan and that looks especially attractive to him, he will take it in his live account. He knows the value of the method and his trading plan, but given that he and his wife have several children, he isn't ready put himself under the pressure of leaving his practice and having to trade every day.

We have another client, Greg, who is a network technician and who is in more of a hurry to learn to trade live. He just put himself on a regiment of getting up three times a week to trade the London morning session. It's not hard for him to go to bed at 6 p.m. EDT three days a week and to get up at 2 a.m., an hour ahead of the London opening. He started out trading micro contracts and is now moving up to trading mini contracts. We know he has discipline and is a good listener because he is more concerned with the consistency of his regimen and working on improving his trading plan than he is with moving up to trading bigger contracts, which is what most people will do after even a hint of success. Greg is in it for the long haul. He knows the value of sticking to his trading plan and the danger of greed and haste. He also knows that if he can make just a few percentage points a week, or even a month, on a regular basis and keep his draw-downs even smaller, he will have no problem finding work as a trader.

With the advent of automatic percentage allocation management module accounts, also known as PAMMs, and leader–follower accounts, where an individual trades her own account and whatever she does is replicated on a percentage basis in another account for an agreed-upon monthly fee, it's reasonable for a trader who can show statements that reflect a consistent performance to become a money manager and either earn a percentage of the profits for all total funds that brokers raise for her or be paid on a monthly basis per account. Greg may or may not end up going that route, but the idea is an interesting one for him, and it helps him stay grounded by reminding him that the thing that matters most is being profitable at the end of the week, and then again at the end of the month.

Traders who overtrade and then use the excuse "I have to trade bigger because I need to make a living trading my small account" are missing the point that in the world of money management, less is more. Let's take a look at two perspectives and decide which one is better for you to adopt. Both perspectives assume that you have already found a viable trading method that you have confirmed through several months of demo trading in live markets. Trader 1: your job is to show up at your trading desk early and prepared and to make some-where between 2 and 3 percent per week while risking 1 percent per trade on a $5,000 account. Trader 2: your job is to show up at your trading desk early and prepared and to make a living trading a $10,000 account and keeping your risk below 2½ percent per trade. It's very obvious which choice has a higher likelihood of success: Trader 1. It's also obvious who an experienced, risk-conscious investor would entrust with trading funds: again Trader 1.

It would be much easier to make $100 to $150 per week, or even per month, and avoid serious drawdowns on a $5,000 account than to try to make $1,000 or more a week on a $10,000 account. Trader 1 would probably have fewer and smaller drawdowns because he could afford to be much more patient in passing on countertrend trades and waiting for favorable setups, while Trader 2 would be under much greater pressure to perform, which would increase the likelihood of drawdowns and mistakes. By realizing this, you put yourself in a much stronger position to achieve it. By not seeing it and trying to be Trader 2, you put yourself in the position of trying to achieve something that is very difficult, and beyond the capabilities of even the most successful traders. Before you start to trade, you need to have realistic expectations, and the reality is that if you can post consistent, realistic results in your own trading account month in, month out, then year in, year out, let us know about it at www.trading-u.com and we can put you in touch with an investment group that is quite likely to have a need for your services.

Achieving success as a trader starts with your believing that it is going to happen, and it can become so only if you are consistent in your efforts. We look forward to having you visit our archives at Trading-U.com/blog, where we have more than 200 trading articles and commentaries available to increase your knowledge of trading, and ideally make you a better trader.

INDEX

ABOUT THE AUTHORS

Jay Norris is the Chief Market Strategist and host of Live Market Exercise for Clovernest Financial Group in Chicago (www.clovernest.com). He worked on the trading floor of the Chicago Board of Trade throughout the 1980s and 1990s in various roles before moving to the customer side of the business in 2001. He has published several articles about trading in *Technical Analysis of Stocks & Commodities* magazine. Norris is the coauthor of *Mastering the Currency Market*. He is a founder of www.Trading-U.com He resides in Chicago.

Al Gaskill brings nearly 38 years of experience to the world of trading. He is a founder of www.Trading-U.com, and coauthor of *Mastering the Currency Market*. He resides in Florida.